Dee,

May you be rich,
read and share _Echoes from God_

Dee Levens
12-7-12

Echoes from God

For Growing Deep, Growing Strong in the Faith

DEE LEVENS

WESTBOW
PRESS

A DIVISION OF THOMAS NELSON

Scripture taken from the New King James Version. Copyright 1979, 1980, 1982 by Thomas Nelson, inc. Used by permission. All rights reserved.

WestBow Press books may be ordered through booksellers or by contacting:

WestBow Press
A Division of Thomas Nelson
1663 Liberty Drive
Bloomington, IN 47403
www.westbowpress.com
1-(866) 928-1240

Because of the dynamic nature of the Internet, any web addresses or links contained in this book may have changed since publication and may no longer be valid. The views expressed in this work are solely those of the author and do not necessarily reflect the views of the publisher, and the publisher hereby disclaims any responsibility for them.

Any people depicted in stock imagery provided by Thinkstock are models, and such images are being used for illustrative purposes only.
Certain stock imagery © Thinkstock.

Author photo taken by SuZan Alexander.

ISBN: 978-1-4497-6079-3 (sc)
ISBN: 978-1-4497-6078-6 (hc)
ISBN: 978-1-4497-6080-9 (e)

Library of Congress Control Number: 2012913872

Printed in the United States of America

WestBow Press rev. date: 08/13/2012

Contents

Praise Page

Life is a journey. You can only live it once. This is a book that brings the truth of God's Word to discover the true purpose of life from the very beginning of our new life in Christ to the conclusion of this mortal life. Thank you, Darenda [Dee], for a book of inspiration, information, and solid Biblical instruction. *Echoes from God* is a must-read for us all.

—Evangelist Dwight Thompson

I have been the Founder and Pastor of Calvary Cathedral International in Fort Worth, Texas for over forty-eight years. I have known Dee [Darenda] and her husband, Jack, ever since they were married in 1968. They have always stayed consistent in their service and lives for the Lord.
Dee has had a hunger to study and understand God's Word. She has majored on the basics of God's Word that are so needed by believers in our churches today. While many seek the great revelations, they ignore the proven basics of God's Word which lay a strong foundation for all of God's believers. Now God has led Dee to put these basic truths into print.
Any believer will greatly profit from reading this book, *Echoes from God*. I personally recommend that every believer study these practical, studied, proven Bible truths which are the essence of her book. This is a mini Bible college education. God's best is yours. I encourage you to read, study, and be blessed as I have been by reading *Echoes from God*.
Echoes from God is so in line with what Paul wrote to Timothy, "Study to shew thyself approved unto God, a workman that needeth not to be

ashamed, rightly dividing the word of truth (2 Tim. 2:15, King James Version)." The Bible truths work when we do them and we believe them.

—Dr. Bob Nichols, Founder and Pastor of Calvary Cathedral International, Fort Worth, Texas

I have had the honor of knowing Dee Levens since 1994. When I became the pastor of Faith Temple, in Killeen, Texas, in 2003 I was already keenly aware of her passion for souls. Dee presented me with her desire to teach new believers how to grow deep and strong in their faith, and I agreed whole-heartedly. The Growing Deep, Growing Strong class was born and countless new believers were established in their faith. I am thrilled that the curriculum developed and written by this master teacher is now available in book form. *Echoes from God* is a powerful tool for all new Christians, and serves as a great Christian education curriculum for churches. I also recommend mature believers to read it every few years for a *refresher course* in what we believe and why we believe it.

—Scott Hoxworth, Senior Pastor, Faith Temple, Killeen, Texas

Acknowledgments

I am grateful to the Lord for giving to me the chapters contained in *Echoes from God*. You see, I have truly struggled with who the author of this book is. Yes, technically I am the author, but let me explain my struggle to you. First, the majority of each chapter is built upon Scripture—God's Word. Second, the Lord gave me all the ideas and stories in the book as I studied and prepared myself to teach God's Word. I really cannot take much credit for them. Finally, this book is printed on paper that came from one of God's trees! You see, I cannot find a single thing in this book I can take sole credit for. My husband, Jack, said I should call the book *Echoes from God* because everything I wrote was simply what I heard from God. He is right!

Even the subtitle of the book did not come from me. My pastor of several years, Pastor Scott Hoxworth, named my Sunday school class "Growing Deep, Growing Strong in the Faith." It just seemed natural to keep the class name as the subtitle of the book, and I believe the subtitle explains what the book is all about: growth. Writing *Echoes from God* has been a learning process for me personally. I have a very patient husband who has always allowed me the space and time to study and write. I will always be grateful for his constant encouragement. In addition, I have two very supportive daughters and sons-in-law, Neil and Janene Graeff and Jonathan and Darla Snead, who have always been cheerleaders for my many activities. Even my six grandchildren, Nathan and Loren Snead and Matthew, Madison, Michael, and Malachi Graeff, have shown me great support with their love.

But there have been so many people who have helped me to get *Echoes from God* in print. First, Pastors Bob Miller and Scott Hoxworth in Killeen,

Texas, both encouraged me to teach the "Growing Deep, Growing Strong in the Faith" Sunday school class, which ultimately led me to write *Echoes from God*. Additionally, my dear friends Larry and Marcia Robinson, who served as my class secretaries, were always there with a word of encouragement to write more. They had no idea, and I certainly did not either, that my weekly curriculum would one day be in print. Reverend Ed Willis also served as my personal cheerleader, always encouraging me to pursue the publishing of this book.

I wanted to make very sure the material I wrote was aligned to the Word of God. I was also concerned about whether the material would be effective if it were used by others. Mrs. Sara Watson, another great Sunday school teacher at our church, began to take my material and use it to teach the same class in the early church service while I continued to teach it in the second service. We met several times to discuss the material, and I often made changes based upon her findings and discussions with her students. Thank you, Mrs. Watson, for being willing to test the material with me.

Reverend Josh Watson gave me valuable input on Holy Communion, and I have enjoyed sitting under his teaching and preaching on several occasions. My sister, Darlene Levens, was a great support, as she also took much of the material and read it for accuracy. Her expertise was invaluable to me! Pastor Paul Moore of Rogers, Texas, has helped me with the alignment and content of the book as well.

My dear missionary friends, Steve and Betty Bishop, were great sounding boards for me. They have so much wisdom about the Word of God, and we have enjoyed hours upon hours of conversation about the Lord and His grace for our lives.

The Lord has once again taught me that He never asks us to take on a task that appears to be bigger than our skill level without providing us with a great cloud of witnesses all around us. I have been supported at every turn, and I am grateful to all those who helped for all of their kindness. I have benefited greatly from having each of you in my life.

Preface

Writing *Echoes from God* has been a journey that began many years ago when I became an adult Sunday school teacher. My pastor asked me to teach the new converts class in our church, which was an honor for me. We did not have a class quite like that at the time, and we felt it was needed. However, as I searched for material that would fit the needs of my new class, I discovered I would have to purchase several different books because none of them seemed to cover all the topics I wanted to teach to my students. Thus, I decided to write my own Sunday school lessons based upon what I perceived God wanted me to teach to the new converts in my fast-growing class. Each week, I got my cup of coffee, my Bible, and a notepad and went to a quiet place to write out the next Sunday's lesson. There were weeks when it took hours to pull together a simple rough draft to serve as the curriculum. It was most often written in a bullet format with simple phrases, and the lesson was always based upon multiple Scripture references. After all, the Word of God was what I wanted to share with the students, so my lessons were primarily a listing of Scriptures that pertained to each topic I felt the Lord had given to me.

My pastor and I decided that I would teach the class as a twelve-week rotational cycle, and then the students would move into one of our other Sunday school class offerings. However, I began to find that instead of losing students, I was recycling students while continuing to receive new students as more and more came to know the Lord as their personal Savior.

In addition, my pastor soon realized it was a great class for new members to attend so they could learn what we as a church believed. If, after going through the class cycle, they agreed with the concepts and beliefs shared, they were invited to join the church.

This type of rotational teaching, which kept me constantly rewriting and refining the material to become more of a true curriculum for the students, continued for several years. As the refining process continued, I took to heart the questions and concerns of the various new converts and new members, many of whom, I might add, had been believers for many, many years. I was busy trying to write the material so it would be useful for nonbelievers, new believers, and more mature believers. Each week I refined the lessons, knowing I would have several students who were recycling them with me for the fourth or even the eighth cycle! I wanted these students to have fresh manna for the day. They were the main people who kept me going back to the Lord for more Scriptures, concepts, and ideas each week.

Then one morning about two years ago, I felt awakened by the Lord. He impressed upon me that I needed to convert the Sunday school curriculum into a book and have it published. I had grown quite comfortable with the lessons' format and informal speech. I felt panicked because I thought that now I had to turn this material into a *book*! I asked the Lord just how I was supposed to do that. I did not feel qualified to write a book. After all, I had just been a Sunday school teacher of over forty years. The Lord spoke to my spirit that I needed to write the book as though I were speaking to my class.

So welcome to my class! As you read this book, be aware that it was written with you in mind. Whether you are a believer or a nonbeliever, it does not matter. I wrote this book because the Lord asked me to. I know He knew you were going to pick this book up one day, and He has guided me with Scriptures to share how much He loves you all throughout this book. Even if you have been a believer for over fifty years, as I have, then read this book with hungry eyes for more of His Word, and know that He knew you were going to be reading this book. He has something to share with you too.

I am often asked how I think this book could best be used. I personally think it is best used as a study tool for an individual or a group. If you are wondering about God's love for you, you will find many answers that will help guide you closer to Him.

As believers, sometimes it is difficult for us to share our Christian witness with others. I trust you will benefit from the study of this book because it is filled with examples of both personal and visual images God has given me. I believe you will be able to apply these stories to the lives of many others along your way. Use the examples in my book as you witness to others.

Let's begin, *class*, shall we? Turn to chapter 1.

A Word of Greeting

I want to welcome you into a journey of growth in God's Word as you read and study *Echoes from God*. You will want to have your Bible handy for the Scripture references. I have used only the New King James Version of the Bible all throughout the book. I have written out most of the Scriptures I refer to for your convenience. However, there will be a few references that I will refer to in the body of the text, or they may be simply listed under the subheadings. Not all of the Scriptures have been printed out within the body of the work. If you are like me, you will also want to have a highlighter and a notepad handy so you can write comments for future study. Use this book as a personal study book for growth in your Christian faith. Whether you are a Christian or not, I believe this book was written just for you.

Echoes from God is written in chronological order, beginning with repentance, then salvation, etc. Some of the chapters could have been placed in a different order depending upon the view of the reader. Because the chapters are written by topic, I have often restated comments, Scriptures, and stories to help emphasize a particular topic.

I have also given an opportunity for you to ponder on reflective questions at the end of a few of the chapters. Once again, this is given as a tool to provoke personal thinking about your own spiritual growth in the Lord.

᷾ *Chapter 1* ᷾

Repentance – Forerunner to Salvation

Introduction
Matthew 3:1-6; 2 Peter 1:11; Romans 10:9-13; Isaiah 64:6

We will begin by looking at the purpose of John the Baptist. He served an important role of preparing people's hearts to receive Jesus as their Lord. John was sent to teach a new message—one of repentance and giving one's allegiance to the Lord. Up to this point in time, people went regularly to the temple to bring their sacrifices for sin to God. These sacrifices served only to cover their sins, not to forgive them. John prepared the people to repent and change their ways so the pure, sacrificial Lamb of God could enter their lives as their Lord and Savior. John's message of repentance was contrary to what the people were used to hearing. They were accustomed to weighing the size or type of sacrifice needed against the specific sins they had committed. A big sin might require a certain sacrifice while another sin might require a lesser sacrifice. This was their way of life until John the Baptist entered the scene.

They knew nothing about spiritual repentance or serving Jesus as their *Lord* and Savior. They also did not know about the concept of spiritual grace and mercy! John the Baptist was a critical introduction to the *way of the Lord*. John showed the people a new way to serve Jesus as their Lord.

When I say *Lord*, I think of someone I serve under (whether by choice or not). The people had been serving under the "lord" of the law that was handed down to them for generations from Moses, who received it from God. John had to prepare the people's hearts to accept a new Lord in their lives. They were used to man's way because it is based upon works, but Jesus was coming on the scene to announce that their works were never going to be good enough for them to enter into heaven. He came preaching on faith, grace, and mercy. John had to get the people ready to accept Jesus as *Lord* of their lives. Until they were ready to follow Jesus, they could not have a new and free life in Christ. Jesus was about to teach the people a whole new life and even a new form of justice. It would be very different from the justice they knew.

John the Baptist was the forerunner for Jesus Christ. His purpose was to prepare the people for the way of the Lord. John preached a sermon on repentance (Matt. 3:1-6). Jesus preached a sermon of love, forgiveness, and acceptance (Matt. 5). We must be willing to search our own lives and submit them to the Lord—just as we are. We cannot work or buy (as was the case of old) our way into salvation or perfection. Christ takes us just as we are. All of our righteousness is as filthy rags in the sight of God (Isa. 64:6). We must recognize we are not clean and we are missing the purpose for living when we do not know Christ as our personal Savior.

John preached on repentance. But what does repentance mean to you and me? To me repentance means to stop, possibly even with great remorse, doing what we feel is wrong. When we turn from something, then I would reason the reverse must also be true. We are turning to something when we repent. For example, if I decide I am going on a diet and refuse to eat sweets or sugars, I may turn to an alternative sweetener to satisfy my craving for sugar. Not only did I turn from something, but in so doing, I chose what to turn *to* as well.

With the concept of turning from and to, we also need to understand *turning to* does not always lead to salvation. There are some who turn from their wicked ways (as they see it) to simply become better people. Although that is good, it does not produce salvation. However, when we turn from our own ways with a repentant heart and *turn to* Jesus to become our Lord *and* Savior, then we are ready to receive salvation. Jesus becomes both Lord *and* Savior of our lives. First we must acknowledge our own willingness to submit our life under His rule and His kingdom. Then and only then are we ready to experience salvation. Salvation is still received according to the Scriptures, as found in Romans 10:9-13, which we will discuss in more depth in chapter 2.

I have had the sweetest and most-well intended parents bring their erring son or daughter to the altar and tell me the child wants to get saved. Well, first of all, at that point the child will probably be obliged to do or say just about anything the parent says because he or she has been dragged to the altar. But unless the child truly wants to *turn from* his or her ways and *turn to* Jesus, there is no salvation. The parents may leave the altar thinking that now things will be better because their child accepted Jesus. Reality is most likely the child only repeated the sinner's prayer but his heart was not prepared to *"make straight the way of the Lord."*

Repentance and salvation are closely tied together, yet they can be worlds apart!

What does "make straight the way of the Lord" mean to you? What is the "way of the Lord"? These were the issues John the Baptist was sent to tell the people about. He understood the *"way of the Lord" was* a life of love and forgiveness, of commitment, of obedience to the Word of God, and much more. As Lord of your life, Jesus will show you His way. It is very different from the way of the world. When you choose to serve under the leadership of Jesus Christ, you open yourself up to a life filled with joy, peace, and contentment like you have never experienced. However, those who choose to stay in their own way will continue to experience anxiety, bitterness, hatred, jealousy, and a long list of grief that only their current lord (Satan) can bring to them.

Why Do We Need to Repent?

Luke 16:13; Ezekiel 18:29-32

You might ask, "Why do I have to repent?" You might even want to say something like, "I'm a good person. I treat people fairly, and I don't see how a loving God would possibly send me to hell." Without repentance, there is no turning away from the way you are living right now, even if you have personally justified your life as spiritually acceptable. You must repent (in the truest sense of turning from your own way and turning toward Jesus) to prepare your spiritual being for the infilling of the Lord in your life. When Christ enters your life, He expects you to serve only Him. You cannot serve both God and man (Luke 16:13). Being a good person will never be good enough, as we will see in this chapter. The reverse is also true; you are never bad enough to prevent you from repenting and experiencing salvation.

Ezekiel 18:29-32 tells us we need to repent so our own iniquities will not be our ruin. How awful it would be if we chose to continue to live in such a state of wickedness that it would tear us down until we were worthless to our fellow man and to ourselves! But unless we turn from our own transgressions and turn toward God, that will be our very end—our ruin.

Ezekiel 18:30 says, "Repent, and turn from all your transgressions, so that iniquity will not be your ruin." Unless we repent, we will continue to go in the wrong direction. But you say, "I can be better. I don't need to go through the confession of my sins." You are partly correct. The Lord does not demand we recall every sin we have ever committed and bring them to the altar of forgiveness. He knows we cannot possibly recall every evil thought or deed we have had or done since birth! He does want us to come to Him with a repentant spirit—a spirit that is willing to acknowledge our sins, stop committing these sins, and turn toward Him. He knows you must choose whom you will serve. You cannot continue in the same path you were on prior to salvation. No matter how good a person you were prior to accepting Christ, He will always be challenging you to grow. That growth as He leads you will always be to your benefit in your Christian walk with the Lord, but it all starts with a repentant spirit.

We All Must Repent

Romans 3:23; Mark 1:1-4; Matthew 3:1-6; Luke 13:1-5; Philippians 3:18-19

No one is a "worse" sinner than another. We *all* must repent and turn from our own ways. In Romans 3:23, Jesus says, "For all have sinned and fall short of the glory of God." This Scripture includes the murderer, the thief, the liar, the sweet little grandmother who bakes cookies for all the folks in the neighborhood, and the little boy who helps others day in and day out! It includes us *all*. We will all have a different prayer of repentance, but we will all have one. One sin that is common to everyone is the sin of wasted time. We have all wasted days and years by not knowing Him. We have all lost valuable time of service and dedication to the work He has prepared for our individual lives. We have all shortchanged our personal lives by wasting days spent without Him as our heavenly Father. What a common shame for us all.

How can we *prepare the way of the Lord and make His paths straight?* In Mark 1:1-4, the Scriptures refer to John the Baptist as the one who was sent to prepare the way of the Lord and to make His paths straight. Now, two thousand–plus years later, how do we do this on our own? We do not have to do it on our own! The Lord sent the Holy Spirit ahead of us to search us out, teach us, and guide us into all understanding of what we are to do and say to come into alignment with Him. It is a process He will carry us through as we grow in faith in the Lord. The first step, however, is to *stop* what we are doing that we know to be wrong because the Holy Spirit has already revealed it to us. Then we must acknowledge Jesus as our Lord and Savior. Please recall I stated repentance and salvation are closely tied together. Repentance is the spiritual attitude in which you will pray the prayer of salvation. (We will study more on salvation in chapter 2.)

Luke 13:5 says, "I tell you, no; but unless you repent you will all likewise perish." We will never experience life without first repenting (turning from our own ways and turning to Christ as our Lord). It is a fact that if we do not repent, we cannot have life; we will perish. Proverbs 21:15 reminds us, "It is a joy for the just to do justice, but destruction will come to the workers of iniquity." Philippians 3:18-19 says, "For many walk, of whom I have told you often, and now tell you even weeping, that they are the enemies of the cross of Christ: whose end is destruction, whose god is their belly, and whose glory is in their shame—who set their mind on earthly things." We must choose whom we will follow. If we choose not to follow Christ, we will stay in our iniquities and thus will be our own ruin.

"God Can't Love Me; I'm too Bad"
John 3:1-17; Matthew 20:28; Mark 10:45; 1 Timothy 2:6; Psalm 103:10-12

John 3:16-17 states, "For God so loved the world that He gave His only begotten Son, that whoever believes in Him should not perish but have everlasting life. For God did not send His Son into the world to condemn the world, but that the world through Him might be saved."

It is amazing that we so often leave out verse 17, "For God did not send His Son into the world to condemn the world, but that the world through Him might be saved." Always remember that Jesus served as our ransom. If He was our ransom, then we must have been held in bondage against our will. If He was willing to go to the cross for you, then you must be worth a great deal to Him. He values you!

The Lord gave me a vision one day of John 3:17 that revealed a depth of His love that I had not previously known. Pretend with me that you are a good parent who has a child you dearly love. From the time the child was very young, you have tried to prepare him with all the safety rules that will ultimately keep him safe; if he follows these simple rules you have taught him. You tell him not to speak to strangers, do not take candy from strangers, do not get into cars with people you do not know, etc. Well, one day in the park a stranger comes up to your little child and begins to speak with him. The stranger convinces your child to take some candy, and before you know it, he has vanished from your sight! He has been kidnapped! A very costly ransom note is eventually delivered to you. The kidnapper took your child only to hurt you. You are the one the kidnapper hates, and therefore he was out to hurt you by stealing your child. You, the loving parent, will pay the price! Now when the child is freed, do you think the first thing you would do is to grab the child and begin to punish him for being disobedient to his rules? No, the parent will grab the child up with open arms and love on him.

We so often read John 3:16, "For God so loved the world that He gave His only begotten Son that whoever believes in Him should not perish but have everlasting life." But John 3:17 actually tells us the reason for the *love*: "For God did not send His Son unto the world to condemn the world, but that the world through Him might be saved." We are not condemned by God, for without Christ we are condemned already. Instead we are saved by Christ because God loved us enough to pay the highest ransom to have us returned to Him. We were kidnapped, but now we are freed by the blood of Christ upon the cross. However, until we truly believe we are free through Jesus and claim Him as our Savior, we remain in our kidnapped state. How sad it is to remain in a life we do not have to have! (See Matt. 20:28; Mark 10:45; 1 Tim. 2:6.) Oh, how it must hurt the father's heart to know his child will not walk away from the kidnapper!

There is one other scenario God shared with me about John 3:16-17. Have you ever played a game of chess? I am not very good at it, but I do know each piece has a specific set of rules attached to it. The ultimate finish is to say, "Checkmate," declaring that you have your opponent's king in a place where he cannot move without being taken by you. At this point, you win. I also know the pawn is an expendable piece. It is the first piece you usually give up to get what you want. Now with that in mind, think of this: Satan sees each of us as pawns—*but* God sees us as kings! Satan is willing for each of us pawns to be thrown away so he can get at God, but God is not willing for any of us to perish. He sees us as kings, and we are to be valued.

God has *not* dealt with us according to our transgressions. He has dealt with us out of love and mercy and grace. He loves us with an undying love, as only a parent can love a child. Psalm 103:10-12 says, "He has not dealt with us according to our sins, nor punished us according to our iniquities. For as the heavens are high above the earth, so great is His mercy toward those who fear Him; as far as the east is from the west, so far has He removed our transgressions from us."

Repentance Is Required for Forgiveness
1 John 1:9; Psalms 32:5, 51:1-2, 10-12

Jesus makes it clear that He is willing and able to forgive us of our sins. However, He also makes it clear that He expects us to bring our sins to Him for forgiveness. First John 1:9 says, "If we confess our sins, He is faithful and just to forgive us our sins and to cleanse us from all unrighteousness." We often hold back on confessing our sins to Him simply because we feel they are too bad! Those sins are the very ones we must confess to Him. Those are the sins the Holy Spirit has brought before your remembrance to ask the Lord to forgive you of. Those are the sins that are tormenting you! They are the ones that are acting like a brick wall between you and your relationship with Christ.

Jesus says to confess your sins and He will cleanse you from all of them. Does that mean He will make everything in your life that is bad disappear and suddenly everything will be new and wholesome again? In the spiritual world, yes; in the physical world, no. In the spiritual world, Jesus said He would cleanse us from all of our unrighteousness. In the physical world we live in, it is necessary for us to cling to His promises and *know* He said we were cleansed and forgiven. We must walk by faith in His promises. We must not condemn ourselves once we have asked Jesus to forgive us. Sometimes we are our own worst enemies in these areas of our faith walk. We continue to doubt that it is possible that anyone—especially a pure and righteous God—could possibly forgive us of the horrible deeds or words we have done or spoken in the past. But He does!

King David said, "I acknowledge my sin to You, and my iniquity I have not hidden. I said I will confess my transgressions to the Lord, and You forgave the iniquity of my sin" (Ps. 32:5). King David had much to confess before the Lord. It was keeping him awake. He was troubled because of the many sins he had committed. He had murdered, committed adultery, and lied. He had much to confess! No wonder he said, "And my sin is always before me" (Ps. 51:3). He asked the Lord to "blot out my transgressions. Wash me thoroughly from my iniquity, and cleanse me from my sin" (Ps. 51:1-2).

There may come a time in your life when you believe you have gone too far into sin to turn back. King David may have thought that, but he still called out to the Lord anyway! "Create in me a clean heart, O God, and renew a steadfast spirit within me. Do not cast me away from Your presence, and do not take Your Holy Spirit from me. Restore to me the joy of Your salvation, and uphold me by Your generous Spirit" (Ps. 51:10-12).

Repent – for the Remission of Sins
Luke 3:3; Hebrews 10:17; Acts 2:38, 3:18-26; Romans 3:23

According to Scripture, once you repent of your sins, you release them to Jesus. You are to repent and be baptized into the family of God. (See Luke 3:3.) Your sins will not follow you in your spiritual life. Although you may continue to see the effects of your past sins upon yours or someone else's life, the sin itself has been forgiven you by Jesus. He holds no grudges against your past because He does not ever recall it to His or your memory again. Hebrews 10:17 states, "Their sins and their lawless deeds I will remember no more." How can He recall to your remembrance what He cannot remember? Thus, when your past sins are brought back into your memory, remember this: they did not come from the Lord.

Romans 3:23 states, "For all have sinned and fall short of the glory of God." God used the words "all have sinned." He does not say some or most have sinned. The word *all* is complete, total, and all inclusive. *No* one is left out of this Scripture. The good, the bad, and the ugly are all included in this Scripture. No matter what category you believe you belong in, you still belong in the "all have sinned" category. Therefore Acts 2:38 says, "Repent, and let everyone of you be baptized in the name of Jesus Christ for the remission of sins; and you shall receive the gift of the Holy Spirit." God has made provisions for everyone who repents and is baptized in the name of Jesus that they will not only see eternal life and forgiveness but will also be eligible to receive the gift of the baptism in the Holy Spirit. (See chapter 7 for more on the baptism in the Holy Spirit.)

Who wants to go about continuing to live a lie? When we say we have no sin or we are okay with not having repented and accepted Jesus as our personal Savior, we live a lie. We are *not* okay. We are doomed! We are still sitting in bondage by our own choice. He has already paid the ransom price for our redemption and our freedom. Why would we not want to step outside of our bondage and into our freedom? Acts 3:18-26 says, "But those things which God foretold by the mouth of all His prophets, that the Christ would suffer, He has thus fulfilled. Repent therefore, and be converted, that your sins may be blotted out . . . To you first, God, having raised up His Son Jesus, sent Him to bless you, in turning away every one of you from your iniquities."

The Kingdom of Heaven Is at Hand
Matthew 3:1-2, 4:17; 13; John 3:3

John the Baptist preached a sermon of repentance for the remission of sins. Matthew 3:2 says, "Repent . . . for the kingdom of heaven is at hand." Jesus preached about the coming of the kingdom of heaven (see Matt. 13). He preached about forgiveness and new birth (John 3:3). Once Jesus completed His experience of forty days in the wilderness, He began His ministry of preaching the gospel of salvation. Matthew 4:17 says, "From that time Jesus began to preach, and to say, repent: for the kingdom of heaven is at hand." The kingdom of God is knocking on your spiritual heart today, seeking to give you freedom from the guilt and transgressions that keep you awake at night—the transgressions that cannot be uttered to anyone! He stands ready to cleanse you from all unrighteousness.

When you bring a spirit of repentance before the Lord, He hears your prayer and comes to change your life. In our next chapter, we will study more on salvation. I challenge you to follow through and go beyond repentance to salvation! A new life awaits you in Christ Jesus.

Reflections

1. If I turn from something, then I must be turning to something. It is my choice to turn to salvation rather than just being a better person.
2. God did not send His Son to condemn me for my sins but rather to save me and set me free from the guilt of my sins (John 3:16-17).
3. Being a good person is not good enough for my salvation. I must repent and turn to Jesus to receive salvation.
4. I thought I was too bad for God to love me! What a revelation! He loves me just like I am, and He wants me to repent and turn toward Him for a new and fresh life in Him.

— Chapter 2 —

Salvation

Introduction

I believe salvation is a spiritual birth. It gives a person life within his or her physical being. Salvation brings deliverance from the power of sin. As we will study in this chapter, salvation is an action word. The act of salvation requires an individual to believe in Jesus, to confess Him as the Son of God, and to believe God raised Jesus from the dead; then and only then will a person be saved. As we learned in chapter 1 on repentance, the individual must also come to Christ with a repentant spirit. Salvation is not difficult; it is designed by God to allow even young children to come to Christ and receive Him as their personal Savior. We adults often try to make the act of salvation difficult and tedious. Let us look at what Christ says about salvation and the simplicity of it.

The Law
Exodus 20:1-17

God gave Moses the Ten Commandments, and they became the law to which man was to measure up. Big problem! No one could measure up to the law. Therefore, we were a needy people. We could never be good enough for salvation.

Man was not under grace; he was to be obedient to the law. In the New Testament, you see countless times when man is to live by faith. You do not see where man is to live by the Ten Commandments. The Ten Commandments were not done away with in the New Testament period of grace; they were perfected through Christ's love being lived out through each of us.

Need of Salvation
Romans 3:10, 23; John 3:3

Romans 3:23 tells us, "For all have sinned and fall short of the glory of God." That *all* have sinned is pretty much an open and shut case. How could we, no matter how good we are, escape this Scripture? We are all in need of salvation. There are none of us who can glory in his or her own salvation. We must come through Jesus. We have all fallen short.

"As it is written: 'There is none righteous, no, not one'" (Rom. 3:10). We may do all the right things in the sight of man. We may rise to the top of our career ladder, yet if we have not accepted Jesus Christ as our personal Savior, we are not saved. Why? Because the Bible clearly states that none are righteous.

We cannot escape it. We will never be good enough on our own to be able to step into heaven without the new spiritual birth of Jesus Christ in our lives. He is our cleansing and our covering to come before the throne room of God. John 3:3 states, "Jesus answered and said to him, 'Most assuredly, I say to you, unless one is born again, he cannot see the kingdom of God.'"

Works Aren't Good Enough
Romans 3:27-28; Ephesians 2:8-9

I want to try to draw you into an "ah-ha" moment by discussing the sweet little old grandma who bakes cookies for all the children up and down the street. She is so sweet, and she never speaks an unkind word or performs an unkind deed. Now let's look at a person who murdered someone. Let us look at his character of hatred and bitterness. I ask you, which one is going to heaven? Some would say the grandma will surely go to heaven. This is a good time to ask yourself if you believe being good is good enough for salvation.

Romans 3:27-28 says, "Where is boasting then? It is excluded. By what law? Of works? No, but by the law of faith." The Bible states salvation is not of works, lest anyone should boast (Eph. 2:9). That is good news, especially if you do not have the means to do an overabundance of good works that can be seen by man. Even then, when will you have committed enough good works to be good enough? What if you were to die young? Would you have accumulated enough good works to cover yourself? Who would be the judge to decide if you had performed enough good works to merit salvation? Get the picture?

Ephesians 2:8-9 says, "For by grace you have been saved, through faith, and not of yourselves; it is the gift of God, not of works lest anyone should boast." We have been saved because of God's grace toward us. It is that simple. The New Testament men and women are to live by faith, which brings in mercy and grace into our lives. How blessed we are!

Jesus Was Not Sent to Condemn You
John 3:16-17; Psalm 103:10-12

John 3:16-17 says, "For God so loved the world that He gave His only begotten Son, that whoever believes in Him should not perish but have everlasting life. For God did not send His Son unto the world to condemn the world, but that the world through Him might be saved."

You will recall the vision I related in chapter 1 on repentance that God gave me one day of John 3:17. It has totally changed my life. You are not condemned by God; you are saved by Christ because God loved you enough to pay a high ransom to have you returned to Him. You were kidnapped, but now you are freed by the blood of Christ upon the cross. However, until you truly believe you are freed through Jesus and claim Him as your Savior, you remain in your kidnapped state. You have a Father who loves you so much that He gave His only Son for you, but He has left the choice up to you to choose either freedom or bondage!

Knowing God did not send His Son into the world to condemn you should begin to make you feel a sense of freedom. Satan wants you to think you are not worthy of God's love, but God has loved you with all He has—His Son.

The Truth Shall Set You Free!
John 8:32

Understanding God's love for you and knowing He does not come to condemn you is freedom! If you believe in Christ, because of who Christ is, you can walk away from Satan, and *then* you will be truly free! However, until the time comes when you truly believe Jesus is the Son of God who came to this earth, born of a virgin birth, lived a sinless life, died for your sins, and rose again to live in heaven with God, His Father, you will never be free. These are beliefs you must take as your own for Jesus' blood to be applied to you personally. Once you believe in Him, you will feel a freedom that will sweep across your very being, and it will compare to no other feeling. It will be a sense of *life* you have never felt before. Jesus brings life to your spirit (which was dead). Salvation is synonymous with birth—spiritual birth. Jesus said, "And you shall know the truth, and the truth shall make you free" (John 8:32).

How Do I Accept Christ into My Heart?
Romans 10:9-13, 15

Jesus made salvation so simple that even a small child can be born into His heavenly kingdom. In fact, Romans 10:15 states, "Assuredly, I say to you, whoever does not receive the kingdom of God as a little child will by no means enter it." This Scripture does not mean that once we become adults, we are no longer eligible for salvation. No—instead it means we must put off all the traditions and layers of bureaucracy we tend to add to our lives so we can receive Christ. As we get older, we begin to deal more with pride, rules, regulations, man's knowledge, etc. We begin to concentrate on the law and our works. We begin to judge one another according to our own established values. None of these are the guidelines by which Christ declares we are saved. He has established a simple set of steps to follow that will lead you directly to the throne room of God. No matter what your age, when you follow these steps, sometimes referred to as "The Romans Road," you will be saved.

> Step 1: Confess Jesus as Lord of your life. Romans 10:9 states, "That if you confess with your mouth the Lord Jesus and believe in your heart that God has raised Him from the dead, you will be saved."

> Step 2. Believe in Him and in His death, resurrection, and life. Romans 10:10 states, "For with the heart one believes unto righteousness and with the mouth confession is made unto salvation."

In chapter 1, we learned that repentance must happen prior to salvation. We learned this for a reason. Repentance and salvation are tied to one another, but they are two distinctly different acts. Repentance is man's role, and salvation is from the Lord. You cannot save yourself; you need Christ for your salvation. Therefore, the Romans Road to salvation clearly states that salvation is about believing in Christ and claiming Him as your Lord and Savior. It is not about works, it is not about who you are, and it is not about condemnation. It is all about making Jesus the head of your life from this day forward.

What's Next?
2 Corinthians 5:17; 1 Corinthians 3:16; John 5:24; Matthew 28:16-20; Luke 24:45-49

Now that you have accepted Christ, you have love within you. Remember that God is love. Through His love, you will begin to see the world in a different light. You will begin to understand the Scriptures in a new and meaningful way. The Bible states you are a new being or creature. Second Corinthians 5:17 states, "Therefore, if anyone is in Christ, he is a new creation; old things have passed away; behold, all things have become new."

When you confessed Jesus Christ as your personal Savior, you did more than just say some words like, "Dear Jesus, please come into my heart." No, you did much more! You see, when you accept Jesus Christ as your personal Savior, He sends the Holy Spirit—the Spirit of God—to dwell within your being. You are no longer alone in this world. You are the temple of the Holy Spirit. Jesus clearly states this in 1 Corinthians 3:16, "Do you not know that you are the temple of God and that the Spirit of God dwells within you?" We are spiritual beings birthed into the kingdom of God, and our earthly bodies will serve as dwelling places of the Holy Spirit. God sent the Holy Spirit to be our comforter, our helper, our guide, and much more, which we will read about in the chapter on the baptism of the Holy Spirit.

The Word of God says you will have everlasting life. John 5:24 says, "He who hears My word and believes in Him who sent Me has everlasting life, and shall not come into judgment." Has anyone ever asked you, "Do you know where you would spend eternity should something happen and you did not have a tomorrow?" Now you have an answer. You are a Christian, a believer. Your name has been recorded in the record books of heaven. You will go to heaven to be with your heavenly Father! How awesome. What a relief to know that you know where you will spend eternity.

However, during this life you will begin to live! You are new, and through His eyes, everything else around you is new too. How could we not go and tell others about Christ's love and redemption for each of us?

Salvation and the freedom it brings to our lives are so wonderful that we need to share the good news of the gospel every chance we get. Jesus directed the disciples to go and make more disciples, teaching them all the great things of the Lord. This is exactly what we as Christians are expected to do. We must also do what Jesus directed the disciples to do. He commissioned them to go! "Go therefore and make disciples of all the nations, baptizing them in the name of the Father and of the Son, and of the Holy Spirit, teaching them to observe all things that I have commanded you; and lo, I am with you always, even to the end of the age. Amen" (Matt. 28:19-20).

Jesus commanded one final thing to His followers just before He ascended into the heavens (after His resurrection): "Behold, I send the Promise of My Father upon you; but tarry in the city of Jerusalem until you are endued with power from on high" (Luke 24:49). Yes, you have the Holy Spirit dwelling within your life the minute you accept Jesus Christ as your personal Savior, but Jesus wanted more for you. You will read in the upcoming chapters about the baptism of the Holy Spirit and see how the Trinity works together to give you all the power you need to be able to live your Christian life victoriously.

—ᖕ *Chapter 3* ᖖ—

Trials and Temptations

Introduction
Hebrews 2:18

As new Christians, we sometimes confuse temptation with sin. Temptation is something you can expect now that you are a Christian. It simply means trying to make one—in this case, the Christian—sin. How and what we do after a temptation has come our way determines whether we have sinned or will sin.

In this chapter, we will take a look at what Christ did when He was tempted by Satan. How did He react, and what did He do when confronted with temptations? Remember, Jesus is our model for every situation in life. Not only did He provide perfect examples for us, but He even told us that once we have gone through some of our temptations, we can expect to be more able to aid others who are going through similar situations in their lives. Hebrews 2:18 says, "For in that He Himself has suffered, being tempted, He is able to aid those who are tempted."

Everything's Going Well
Matthew 3:13-17; Luke 3:21-22

Have you ever thought to yourself, *Boy! Just when things are going so well, something always seems to happen to me."* Let us look at what happened to Jesus right after He received an awesome compliment from God the

Father. Matthew 3:17 says, "And suddenly a voice came from heaven, saying, 'This is My beloved Son in whom I am well pleased.'" God gave this public acknowledgment and compliment to Jesus right after He came up out of the water after being baptized by John the Baptist. It was especially big because everyone around Jesus got to hear what was spoken by God concerning Jesus. What a confirmation! What a spirit lifter. Just imagine if God were to speak audibly in front of all those standing around you that He was pleased with you and you were His child. How much better can it get than that!

Beware of the "If" Word!
Matthew 4:1-11; Luke 4:1-12; Mark 1:12-13; Psalm 91:9; Philippians 2:8-11; Colossians 2:9-10

Jesus surely felt wonderful on that day as His heavenly Father spoke these words over Him in the presence of everyone standing around. But it is important to read on in the Scriptures and see what happened next in Jesus' life. Matthew 4:1 says, "Then Jesus was led up by the Spirit into the wilderness to be tempted by the devil." We see Jesus being complimented by His heavenly Father, and in the next moment, we read He is being led by the Spirit to be tempted! If that had been me standing there, I might have felt like I was on a spiritual roller coaster. Have any of you ever had that feeling of extreme highs and lows in your spiritual journey with the Lord?

Let us look at what happened to Jesus right after He got such a profound compliment from God. We in the natural might think Jesus would have been carried off to some great throne room to be immediately crowned King. After all, the crowd clearly heard God say Jesus was His Son. But no—instead Jesus was led by the Spirit into the *wilderness* for a time of fasting and to be tempted by Satan for forty days and nights. At the end of the forty days, Satan arrived on the scene to tempt Jesus.

Satan seems to make it his business to know our character—to know our strengths and weaknesses. He plays off of what he assumes to be the weakest area in our lives at the time. In this case, he knew Jesus had been fasting forty days and nights and was therefore hungry.

Always be wary when Satan uses the word *if*. It is sure to be a *trap*! It is a dead giveaway! When he can begin to plant seeds of doubt in your spirit, the battle is so much easier for him. He tries to make you doubt your faith in Jesus. Once this doubt has settled into your spirit, Satan has completed what he intended to do because now you will begin to listen to him and question God.

Let us look at the seeds of doubt and temptation Satan tried to use against Jesus. Matthew 4:3 says, "If You are the Son of God, command that these stones become bread." Satan will question your salvation. He will question your relationship to God. Of course Jesus was the Son of God! That should end the conversation right there. When Satan uses the "if" word, we know he is setting us up for some sort of trickery. Have you ever noticed there are times in your Christian walk when you begin to hear a tiny whisper in your spirit: "If you are a Christian, how can this be happening to you?" "If you are a Christian, why do you feel so alone?" These are just two examples of the countless phrases Satan likes to use in his devious speeches. He plants doubt within our spirits to bring confusion. Be careful.

He Starts with the Most Obvious Temptations
Matthew 4:6-11; Philippians 2:8-11; John 8:44

Satan began his temptation at the most obvious place with Christ. He knew Jesus was hungry, and therefore he began by telling Jesus to turn the stones into bread. Think about it: Jesus could have performed that miracle at any point during those forty days of fasting. He did not need Satan to tell Him to do it. There was a reason for the fasting, and Jesus did not bend with Satan's temptation.

Matthew 4:6 states, "Throw Yourself down." Satan wants us to *throw* ourselves down! He wants us to put ourselves in situations that keep us forever in trouble—placing ourselves in paths we know would not be safe for ourselves or others. Remember, Jesus does not perform for Satan. He will not put on a show for Satan. He has nothing to prove to him. Jesus has already proven His power. Once again, Satan uses, "If you are the Son of

God," as he sets Christ up for the next temptation. Note how he continues to try to get Jesus to doubt if He is truly the Son of God. Not only does Satan want us to doubt our salvation, but he also wants us to put ourselves in harm's way.

Always read the *before and after* of a Scripture when it is quoted to you by anyone, especially by Satan! Satan left out a key portion of the Scripture he quoted to Jesus. He left out the *reason* the angels would protect Jesus. Psalm 91:9-11 states, "*Because* you have made the Lord, who is my refuge, even the Most High, *your dwelling place*, no evil shall befall you, nor shall any plaque come near your dwelling; for He shall give His angels charge over you." *Because* you have chosen to serve the Lord as *your* Most High God, He will protect you. The angels will *not* automatically be discharged to go and rescue you just because Satan tells you to tempt God and put yourself in bad situations. No! This protection is promised because of the relationship we have with the Lord.

Matthew 4:7 tells us Jesus' response to Satan: "It is written again, 'You shall not tempt the Lord your God.'" There is nothing Satan offers that even begins to offer a temptation to God. Sometimes we have to remind Satan he is not to tempt God. Always remember that we should never purposefully try to tempt God. We are to trust and serve God but never tempt Him. He will always come through for us without us having to stoop to trying to tempt Him.

In Matthew 4:8-9, Satan showed Jesus all the kingdoms of the world and their glory. Satan tried to trick Jesus into worshipping him once again. Notice Satan had nothing of his own to offer Jesus. All these things already belonged to Jesus. Here we see the "if" word being used once again by Satan: "If You will fall down and worship me." Satan made it sound as though Christ would be left with nothing if He did not fall down and worship Satan. How smooth Satan was to try to use all of Christ's own belongings as though they were his own. What else could he do? He has nothing good of his own to give to us. Satan can only offer lies; he owns them!

I wonder how often we feel as though our careers will be damaged if we do not do what we think the world, or our employer, wants us to do that we know is contrary to God's guidelines for our lives. Maybe you have been told you will never make it on your own. You need this person or that thing to be successful. Look at what Christ had to say about it.

Just Do What Jesus Did
Matthew 4:10; Philippians 2:8-11; Colossians 2:9-10

Jesus said in Matthew 4:10, "Away with you, Satan! For it is written, 'You shall worship the Lord your God, and Him only you shall serve.'" See Philippians 2:8-11, and learn how Jesus has to remind Satan once in a while he too will one day bow before Him. If we go the way of the world, we will still have to come full circle and bow before God. We will bow not only our spirit but also in our will. I would much prefer to give my will to God now and do it His way rather than bowing to Him when it is too late for me.

What a victorious life there is ahead for the followers of Christ!

When we are faced with *ifs* from Satan, we must do as Jesus did. We must tell Satan to get away! You will notice Jesus never carried on long conversations with Satan. It was almost like He did not give him the time of day. Jesus only used the Word of God against Satan, and then when He had enough of his foolishness, He directed him to leave. Jesus gives us two tools to use against Satan. The first is to use only the Word of God against Satan, not your own words. The second is to *direct*, not ask, Satan to leave your presence. Satan does not seem to respond to requests and politeness from us. You must be firm in your command that he leave your presence immediately.

Colossians 2:9-10 states, "For in Him dwells all the fullness of the Godhead bodily; and you are complete in Him, who is the head of all principality and power." Through the blood of Jesus, we are complete and have all authority over Satan! We do not have to listen to Satan. After all, he only lies.

Satan Has Many Tricks!

Romans 10:9-10; Matthew 6:24; Luke 16:13; 1 Corinthians 15:33

When Satan throws out the old, *"You're not saved!"* line at you, just ask yourself the following questions: Did you follow the steps as quoted in Romans 10:9-10? Have you confessed Jesus Christ as your Savior? Have you asked Him to forgive you of your sins? Have you asked Him into your heart? Then trust and obey the Scriptures. Remember, Satan can only offer you lies and trickery.

You cannot serve two masters. That phrase simply means that you can choose to serve Jesus or not. It will always be your choice and no one else's. (See Matt. 6:24 and Luke 16:13.) We are to be careful in the choices we make. There are some choices that can lead us away from the presence of the Lord while others will draw us even closer to the Son of God. These decisions are strictly your choice.

Along those same lines of thought, we must choose whom we associate with and whom we call our close friends. Sometimes we place ourselves in harm's way for temptation to enter into our lives simply by hanging out with the wrong crowd. "Do not be deceived: Evil company corrupts good habits" (1 Cor. 15:33). Only we can emphasize the importance of choosing our close friends wisely. They should be Christians. We can have friends from all walks of life, but those we choose to spend our time with should be people who also serve and love the Lord our God.

But My Temptations Are Too Hard

1 Corinthians 10:13; Hebrews 4:12-16

Have you ever felt terribly alone in your time of temptation? According to God's Word, "No temptation has overtaken you except such as is common to man" (1 Cor. 10:13). When you read this Scripture, you begin to realize that others have gone through similar situations from generation to generation. Although you may feel alone in your struggles, Jesus has already successfully walked this road with many others before you. He can handle your problems as well.

Jesus was "in all points tempted as we are" (Heb. 4:12-16). When the urge swells up within you to say there is no way anyone can possibly understand what you are going through, remember that Jesus was tempted in all points as you are tempted. Jesus successfully bore the temptations to show us how to lead a victorious life through our trials and temptations. Temptations will come our way, but Jesus has modeled for us how to be successful. In addition, we have the right to go before the throne of God and petition for assistance to get us through a particular trial. Jesus will not laugh at you for your weakness; He will totally understand because He has already been there too. He knows there will be hard trials ahead of you.

I Am Worried About It!
Matthew 6:25-34

Let us see if worrying about the situation will help. Read Matthew 6:25-34. It is so easy to allow worry to slip into our lives. Before we even realize it, we are worrying or fretting over something we feel we have no control over. Matthew asked, "Which of you by worrying can add one cubit to his stature?" (Matt. 6:27). Not only do we not grow an inch taller with our worrying, but we might even begin to appear shorter in stature. Have you ever noticed that people who are worrying go about with their heads down and their shoulders slumped over? Their backs even begin to look like they are hunched over with worry as well. I also suspect they have headaches, heartburn—you name it!

There are situations we will find ourselves in that require our trust in the Lord. Trust—not worry—is the key to overcoming doubts and temptations. When we get to the point where we have no obvious solutions, then we need to look at a faith walk with the Lord and rely upon Him for our guidance. In so doing, we must look up, not down; rejoice, not moan and grumble; shout for joy, not fear; and trust, not doubt. Get the idea? Every situation you face, whether a trial, temptation, or test of your faith, all boils down to you simply putting your trust in the Lord.

Trials Bring Blessings and a Witness
2 Corinthians 5:17; James 1:12; Philippians 4:13; Hebrews 2:18

As parents, we sometimes allow our children to take the next step on their own. We are right behind them to catch them before they fall, but they must learn to walk. Sometimes we find certain temptations are no longer temptations through the blood of Jesus. We have conquered that particular temptation. Things we once thought we could not handle (maybe bad language, bad thoughts, etc.) we now find we are no longer tempted by. They no longer bother us. We are new creatures and even begin to think in new ways. (See 2 Cor. 5:17.) The reason is because of the relationship we now have with Christ. That relationship changes everything! We are growing spiritually and overcoming temptations that once caused us to stumble.

The Bible says, "Blessed is the man who endures temptation" (James 1:12). There is a special inner peace we feel when we have successfully overcome a temptation. It is a feeling of victory in knowing who we are in Christ. "I can do all things through Christ who strengthens me" (Phil. 4:13).

Hebrews 2:18 states, "For in that He Himself has suffered, being tempted, He is able to aid those who are tempted." We are also more able to aid those who suffer if we have gone through a similar trial or temptation. We can give His Word and our testimony of God's abiding grace as a witness. We do not go out searching for our next trial or temptation to conquer and have a new testimony! However, we know when Jesus has confidence in us to believe we are ready for the next test, He will allow it only for our good. It is just like the parent who followed behind the young toddler as he began to learn to walk no longer needs to follow the child once he has demonstrated he can walk on his own without falling. However, the parent now knows there are more dangers and temptations ahead for the young child and will be there to protect and guide him through each phase of his young life.

Bear One Another's Burdens
Galatians 6:1-2

We are to pray for and help one another during their times of trials and burdens. Galatians 6:1-2 tells us, "Brethren, if a man is overtaken in any trespass, you who are spiritual restore such a one in a spirit of gentleness, considering yourself lest you also be tempted. Bear one another's burdens and so fulfill the law of Christ." The key phrase here is "in a spirit of gentleness." This is the spirit we are to use with those who are "overtaken in any trespass." Sometimes this is hard for us. We want to force them to stop whatever we believe they are doing wrong and begin to live right *now*! We have no patience for their foolishness! But we are to bear one another's burdens in love and gentleness.

We will all face trials and temptations throughout our Christian walk. We will be faced with many diverse temptations that will test our faith. But Jesus, as always, is the perfect model for us to follow when we are tested. We must be ready to use the Word of God wisely in each situation. God's Word is powerful, and it is guaranteed to bring success with each and every test we face.

Being tested is not a sin. It is what we choose to do with the test that determines whether any sin will come from the temptation. Recall that Jesus was in all points tempted as we will be tempted. Jesus was a man who knew no sin. Temptation is not sin. Once you choose to follow Jesus, do not detour from your decision. Give Jesus your whole life. Do not hold any area back from the Lord. Those areas of our lives we try to hold back are the obvious areas that Satan will pick at time and again to test us.

Food for Thought Questions
Romans 10:9-13

Here are some questions to ponder within your own spirit. Remember, you are not alone. Jesus will be with you every step of the way. He truly understands your concern over your test, but He wants to provide you peace in the midst of the storm.

1. When I'm tempted I feel like . . .
2. When Satan told Jesus, "If you are the Son of God," what do you think were some of the thoughts that may have crossed Jesus' mind at that moment?
3. Do you recall being tempted this past week? Do you feel as though you won this test? Why?
4. How do you *know* you are saved (Rom. 10:9-13)?
5. Why did you go through a particular temptation?

   a. Did you allow yourself to be placed in this situation by your own choice of friends, place, etc.?
   b. Are you being tested because the Lord wants you to experience a deeper walk with Him in this area of your life and He knows you are strong enough to handle it?

— ❧ *Chapter 4* ❧ —

Prayer

Introduction
Psalm 5:1-3

It is very important for us to begin each day with the Lord. King David knew his life depended upon God's safety and protection, forgiveness, peace, and joy. David recognized that without Jesus, he could do nothing. He sang in the Psalms he would begin each day by crying out to the Lord. We should do the same.

> Give ear to my words, O Lord, consider my meditation. Give heed to the voice of my cry, my King and my God, for to You I will pray. My voice You shall hear in the morning, O Lord; in the morning I will direct it to You. And I will look up (Ps. 5:1-3).

Our most important prayer should be the one of salvation. Following are written the steps to salvation. Salvation is the spiritual birth that brings eternal life to us. It ushers in the Holy Spirit for our lives and creates a new and clean spirit for us to have a beautiful relationship with our Lord Jesus Christ.

Salvation
Romans 10:9-13

Although I wrote out the steps to salvation in chapter 2, I believe it is worth reviewing once again as a prayer. Romans 10:9 states, "That if you confess with your mouth the Lord Jesus and believe in your heart that God has raised Him from the dead, you will be saved."

> Step 1 of salvation: You must *confess* Jesus Christ, the Son of God, to be your Savior.
>
> Step 2 of salvation: You must *believe* Jesus died on the cross and was raised from the dead.

Salvation is not a single statement of faith, no more than a marriage vow is the marriage. The vow, whether spoken to your soon-to-be spouse or spoken in prayer to Jesus, must be lived daily in the sight of all who know you. Otherwise, the vow was just a set of pretty words. Salvation is no different. The words spoken to Christ are intended for a lifetime.

After the Salvation Prayer
Exodus 3:14

Now that you have asked Jesus to be your Lord and Savior, you should call upon Him for all your needs, and best of all, you can simply talk with Him as your personal friend or Father. Communication with the Lord is so special and different for each child of God.

I have taught a new converts Sunday school class for years, and one of the more frequent questions I am asked is, "How do I pray?" I finally came up with an answer I feel is as close to defining our everyday prayer as I can get. I tell new converts to speak to Jesus in the form of their need or desire.

For instance, if you go to a counselor, is there a particular way that you speak to him? Do you tell him what is bothering you and let him help you work through your problems? How about a doctor? Do you tell him where it hurts and listen to him tell you what to do for a particular pain? The list goes on. How about a best friend? Do you tell your friend all your secrets, your joys, and your sorrows? Get the idea? Speak to the Lord in your everyday voice as though you were speaking to your counselor, doctor, best friend, or whatever the occasion may be for you at the time of your prayer. Jesus said He is the I AM for all areas of your life (Ex. 3:14). We should pray to the Father for all of our needs, desires, and joys.

The Lord's Prayer for Private Worship
Matthew 6:6, 9-13

The Lord's Prayer (Matt. 6:9-13) is so often quoted and so often not studied by Christians. We frequently miss what Jesus was really telling His disciples when He taught them how to pray. I refer to it as the prayer for our private, personal worship. It is a relationship-building prayer. The Lord stated this was a prayer to pray when you "enter into your closet" or private place of worship (Matt. 6:6). It is not a prayer for the public. It is personal. This is not to say that it cannot be quoted or sung in public, but the purpose was to give guidance to the believer on how to approach the Lord in prayer.

> Our Father in heaven, hallowed be Your name. Your kingdom come. Your will be done on earth as it is in heaven. Give us this day our daily bread. And forgive us our debts, as we forgive our debtors. And do not lead us into temptation, but deliver us from the evil one. For Yours is the kingdom and the power and the glory forever. Amen (Matt. 6:9-13).

Step 1: Recognize whom you are praying to. "Our Father . . ."

Step 2: Recognize His name is holy and to be respected.

Step 3: Recognize we are to desire or long for His kingdom to come.

Step 4: We are to submit to His will for our life just like it is in heaven.

Step 5: Give us this day our daily bread is bigger than food. I believe our *"daily bread" is the Word of God we need for today.* There is a word from God that is intended for your life today. God wants you to desire to have fresh manna from Him on a *daily* basis, not just on Sundays.

Step 6: He continues with the prayer and says, "And forgive us our debts, as we forgive our debtors." This is a conditional portion of the prayer. It can be read, "As I forgive others, God will forgive my debts!" You see, Jesus wants us to forgive the debtor. He did not say the debt; He said debtor, just as we were a debtor to Him. He forgave me, the debtor. When He forgave me, He also saved me, forgave my debts, and set me free! He wants us to do the same for others. That could be different for everyone who owes you, whether it is in financial, emotional, or other areas of your relationship with the debtor.

Step 7: Jesus wants us to pray that we are not led into temptation but delivered from the evil one. Jesus is the one who can fight our battles, and He is the one who can deliver us when we feel tempted.

Step 8: Recognize it is His kingdom and His power and His glory forever— not ours. *Amen.*

The word "amen" means "so be it." When you conclude your prayer with the Lord and end with "amen," you are saying "so be it." You are in agreement with the Lord for the prayer. In addition, it is like you finished the prayer with the phrase, "It's done!" Therefore, when you say "amen," aren't you also saying, "I trust Jesus enough to complete all I carried to Him today in prayer, and He trusts me enough to carry out His Word as He spoke it to me in prayer today as well"? You see, the Lord's Prayer is a powerful guideline for our lives. It is much more than a prayer to be sung in songs and quoted in unison in public arenas. That is all fine, but always recall Jesus has given you a guideline for more than a public tool. He has brought it to a personal level between you and Him.

Prayer to Seek Only Him
Matthew 6:33-34; Malachi 3:8

Matthew 6:33-34 states, "But seek first the kingdom of God and His righteousness, and all these things shall be added to you. Therefore do not worry about tomorrow, for tomorrow will worry about its own things. Sufficient for the day is its own trouble."

When we seek Him first, He has promised He will take care of our needs. Note that this Scripture closely relates to tithing. When a Christian tithes, Jesus has promised to pour out a blessing for him or her. It is hard to seek Jesus first and be called a robber by Him at the same time. Read Malachi 3:8.

How can you honestly say you are seeking Jesus first in your life when you spend all your days and nights worrying about issues? You will always have concerns; if it is not one thing, then it will be another. Jesus knew that when He told you to seek Him first. He desires to take care of you. If you are truly trusting in His Word for your needs, then you can remain more focused on being about the Father's business, and you will not lose your joy while going through whatever issue is at hand.

Prayer for His Return
Mark 13:32-33

"But of that day and hour no one knows, not even the angels in heaven, nor the Son, but only the Father. Take heed, watch and pray, for you do not know when the time is" (Mark 13:32-33).

Once again this Scripture is tied back into the Lord's Prayer, "Your kingdom come." We are to pray for His return. Jesus is coming back for His children, and we are to be watching and waiting. What if you were engaged and were not joyfully awaiting your wedding day? Would you say there might be a relationship problem in such a case?

Prayer for Guidance
Matthew 26:39

Jesus modeled how to pray the tough prayers. He knew no matter what, He was to do the will of His Father. That is to be our ultimate submissive prayer as well. When we are faced with situations we do not want to experience, we must pray just as Jesus did.

Matthew 26:39 states, "He went a little farther and fell on His face, and prayed, saying, 'O My Father, if it is possible, let this cup pass from Me; nevertheless, not as I will, but as You will.'"

Here we see not only a submissive prayer but a prayer of commitment. Jesus modeled what we must do when we are faced with hard times: go to prayer. Jesus sought God, His Father, for guidance. It is interesting to note that this prayer was prayed alone between Jesus and God. He did not go to His disciples, His family, or any other earthly advisors for guidance. There are times when we need to pull away and seek only the face of God, and we need to do it one on one. There are some prayers that only you can pray. After having prayed this tough prayer, even in the most difficult time of His earthly life, Jesus accepted His Father's decision for His direction.

Prayer to Learn
Matthew 11:28-30

Jesus tells us to come to Him when we are burdened. He desires to carry your burdens and for you to take on His yoke. Being yoked to Jesus makes your load seem so much lighter. He carries the heavy end for you!

Matthew 11:28-30 states, "Come to Me, all you who labor and are heavy laden, and I will give you rest. Take My yoke upon you and learn from Me, for I am gentle and lowly in heart, and you will find rest for your souls. For My yoke is easy and My burden is light."

Jesus said, "Take My yoke upon you" as a way of staying connected to Him when times are hard. A yoke simply served to attach two or more animals (or anything else) together. There are times when we need to slip into a yoke with Christ and release our burdens onto His shoulders. He can carry the excess baggage much better than us. When you feel all hunched over with guilt, worry, fear, or anything else, recognize that you are probably not yoked up to Jesus at this time of your life. Go to Him in a submissive prayer, and let Him carry your load. He has already asked you to let Him do it. He hands us the yoke (a symbol of trust), but we must be willing to put it on ourselves.

Prayer to Be in His Presence
Matthew 18:20

One kind of prayer is when we gather together with other Christians and begin to seek Jesus. He assures us He is present! How much more could one want?

Matthew 18:20 tells us, "For where two or three are gathered together in My name, I am there in the midst of them." Pray together as *one* in *unity*. You have really missed a special moment in your life if you have not already experienced the prayer of unity that can be felt while praying with other believers. Seek out prayer partners who will worship the Lord with you.

For Our Material Needs
Matthew 6:25-33

It is so easy to become caught up in worry. If you choose to seek Him first, He will take care of those things that so easily worry you. Do not forget, this goes back to the principle of tithing once again. If you are truly seeking Him first, you are being obedient to His Word.

Matthew 6:25, 33 says, "Do not worry about your life . . . But seek first the kingdom of God and His righteousness, and all these things shall be added unto you." (More will be taught on this principle in the chapter on tithing.)

Prayer for Healing
Mark 9:23; Psalms 23:4, 112:7; John 19:34; Isaiah 53:5; 1 Peter 2:24

We often get "bad reports" in our life. We did not get the job we just knew we were going to get. We did not get the house we thought God had designed for us. We did not like the report the doctor gave us about our blood tests, etc. The reports are endless, but King David understood man's reports are just that—man's. He believed in the one who is able to take care of us from sunup to sundown, and he refused to let man's reports draw him into a state of doubt.

Mark 9:23 states, "Jesus said to him, 'If you can believe, all things are possible to him who believes.'" Psalm 112:7 tells us to not fear a bad report or evil tidings, and in Psalm 23:4, David says we go *through* the valley of the shadow of death. He does not say we stay in the valley.

Your healing is a gift from the Lord. Jesus could have died for your sins without having to endure the beatings and the many stripes that were laid across His body. His blood had to be shed for your salvation, but was it necessary to have taken the stripes? His blood was shed upon the cross when the soldiers pierced His side with the sword. (See John 19:34.) But what about the stripes? He went the extra mile of enduring the stripes for our healing. Oh, how much He must love us to endure all that was required of Him that day. He paid for our salvation and our healing with His own blood and body. Now we must trust Him for the completion of healing within our own bodies.

For Forgiveness
Mark 11:25-26; Matthew 6:14-15, 7:1; Luke 6:37; Romans 14:13; 1 John 1:9; Psalm 51:14-17

Pray to Forgive Others: Mark 11:25-26 says, "And whenever you stand praying, if you have anything against anyone, forgive him, that your Father in heaven may also forgive you your trespasses. But if you do not forgive, neither will your Father in heaven forgive your trespasses."

Matthew 6:14-15 says, "For if you forgive men their trespasses, your heavenly Father will also forgive you. But, if you do not forgive men their trespasses, neither will your Father forgive your trespasses."

Jesus was the model of how to forgive others. He forgave me, and He forgave you, didn't He? Jesus does not like unforgiveness! He dislikes it so much that He instructed us to not stand before Him with unforgiveness in our hearts. We must forgive those who have offended us, no matter how deeply we were hurt by them. Does Jesus forgive a murderer, a liar, a thief, and a cheat? I do not know how badly you were hurt by someone, but I know you will never be able to stand in God's presence and feel His love like you desire to until you have forgiven whoever has hurt you. Forgive and let God handle those who have hurt you. They are, and always were, in God's hands. He is the ultimate judge of them, not us. (See Matt. 7:1; Luke 6:37; Rom. 14:13.)

Pray For Your Own Forgiveness: First John 1:9 says, "If we confess our sins, He is faithful and just to forgive us our sins and to cleanse us from all unrighteousness." It is one thing to ask Jesus to forgive you of your sins, but your prayer life will be greatly hindered if you do not forgive yourself as well. Jesus is our model in everything. If He can forgive us—and He does—then we must follow through with our own forgiveness. You will never find true joy in serving the Lord—or in anything else for that matter—until you receive and give forgiveness.

Pray with the Right Spirit: Psalm 51:14-17 talks about a *broken and contrite heart.* The bottom line is that you must forgive to be forgiven. So often we say things like, "I'll never forgive that person!" You shut the door on God's blessings for your life. He forgives you as His child; He expects you to do the same. Jesus accepts a broken and contrite heart, not a bitter or hardened heart.

For Power from on High
Luke 24:49

"Behold, I send the Promise of My Father upon you; but tarry in the city of Jerusalem until you are endued with power from on high" (Luke 24:49).

Have you sought the infilling of the baptism of the Holy Spirit with the evidence of speaking in other tongues? Jesus pointed the disciples back to Jerusalem to wait and tarry until they were endued with power from on high! He did not say, *"Now if you'd like to, go and be filled."* No! He told them He was sending the Promise of His Father upon them, and they were to tarry, or to wait with anticipation, until they were endued with power from on high. We know we need this power. Man's power alone is not sufficient to fight the good fight of faith. (Refer to chapter 7 on baptism in the Holy Spirit for more insight into this topic.)

For Friendship
Proverbs 18:24

Proverbs 18:24 tells us, "But there is a friend who sticks closer than a brother." There is no sweeter friendship than that which comes from Jesus Christ. He knows how to make you feel loved and appreciated. He knows when you are down and He knows how to pick you up. However, He also knows how to straighten you out and tell it like it is to you, just like any close true friend would do. He is an awesome friend!

Marvel at Him!
Matthew 8:26-27; Exodus 3:13-15; Isaiah 9:6

Matthew 8:27 reads, "So the men marveled, saying, 'Who can this be, that even the winds and the sea obey Him?'" There are times when it is breathtaking just to sit in His presence. He is so great and powerful. He is our Savior, our friend, our Lord, our counselor, our Prince of Peace, and our all-in-all. He is the *great* I AM! (See Exodus 3:13-15.) Jesus is worthy of all our praise. Never miss an opportunity to sit in His presence just to worship Him.

How Do I Speak to Jesus?

I have so often had young Christians in the faith tell me they do not know how to pray. This chapter has shown many aspects of prayer, but there is one piece that still seems to stump so many, and they say to me, "I just don't know what to say or how to say it." I understand that. After all, God is so big, and we are mere people.

As I stated earlier in this chapter, the Lord once showed me we are to talk to Him in the manner of our needs. If you feel you need a counselor, speak to Jesus as though you were sitting in the counselor's office. If you are ill and need a doctor, speak to Jesus and tell Him where it hurts. If you are in need of a financial breakthrough, speak to Jesus as though you were talking to a banker or finance officer. He will meet you at the point of your need. You do not need a special holy voice or well-planned words to speak to Jesus. After all, He hears you every day and at every moment already, so use your everyday language. You do not need special "thees" and "thous" to reach the heart of God.

If you are lonely and need a friend, talk to Him just like you would with your best friend. He understands and carries all your burdens better than a friend could ever do.

Learn to speak to Jesus in the form of your need. He will always listen, and He will never laugh at your humble desire to speak with Him. Remember, He desires a humble and contrite spirit, not a haughty one. He loves you all the more for your attempt at speaking with Him. You have made Him your choice, and He loves you. Speak to Him today.

Take a Moment to Pray

Whatever your need is, whether it is salvation, financial, emotional, or healing, you name it, Jesus desires to hear from you today. Take a moment to enter into your own prayer closet and speak to Jesus in the form of your need. And above all, take time to simply praise Him because He is the King of Kings, Lord of Lords, and the One who loves us most.

—ᢒ Chapter 5 ᢒ—

Water Baptism

Introduction
Mark 1:4, 8; Luke 1:76-79

John the Baptist understood the phrase, "It's all about Him!" John said, "I indeed baptize you with water, but He will baptize you with the Holy Spirit" (Mark 1:8).

John the Baptist was called to go before the Lord: "For you will go before the face of the Lord to prepare His ways, to give knowledge of salvation to His people by the remission of their sins, through the tender mercy of our God, with which the Dayspring from on high has visited us; to give light to those who sit in darkness and the shadow of death, to guide our feet into the way of peace" (Luke 1:76-79).

John the Baptist could not be the salvation of the people, nor did his water baptism save people. John's preaching was to prepare the people for Christ's ways, not man's ways.

John preached a "baptism of repentance for the remission of sins" (Mark 1:4). John was preaching to the people a need to repent (to stop and turn from their own ways) and to look to God for the remission of their sins. When we *know that we know* our sins are forgiven us, then there is a cleanliness that sweeps over us like nothing else can bring into our lives.

Christ came on the scene just months later, and He completed what John the Baptist was only able to lay the groundwork for: salvation by Christ dying on the cross, His resurrection, and His ascension into heaven to be at the right hand of the Father.

*Now, two thousand–plus years later,
what does water baptism mean to us?*

Water Baptism Is . . .
1 John 1:7

Water baptism is an act of obedience on the Christian's part. It is following after Christ's example. It is not the act of salvation; it is the declaration of salvation. Water cannot wash away our sins. Only the pure blood of Christ can cleanse us of our sins. "And the blood of Jesus Christ His Son cleanses us from all sin" (1 John 1:7). It is a statement of your salvation—of your commitment to turn away from your sinful acts, deeds, and thoughts and your desire to openly follow wholly after Christ. It is a statement that is so profound one could compare it to a wedding ceremony. It is the public act of stating once and for all your desire to be forever joined with Christ in both His death and His resurrection, in His ministry, in His love for the people, and in your undivided love for Him.

You can compare your life in this public statement to the burying of your old, sinful life (the act of submersion under the water) to the new life you have received through accepting Christ (the act of raising up out of the water). The minister normally does the baptizing, and he will usually say, "In the name of the Father, the Son, and the Holy Spirit," declaring your Christian name! You are a child of the King!

Does Water Baptism Save Man?
2 Corinthians 5:17; Matthew 3:7-12, 28:19, 20; Ephesians 2:8-9; Mark 1:3

Water baptism is a public statement of a repentant spirit for the remission of your own sins. It means you have given your life of sin to Christ, just as He committed His life to be a ransom for your sins on the cross. It means you are raised up as a new creature and are committed to serve Him all the days of your life (2 Cor. 5:17), just as Christ arose and returned to His disciples, and over five hundred other witnesses, to command us to "go therefore and make disciples of all the nations" (Matt. 28:19). Water baptism means we recognize our salvation comes from Christ alone and not because of anything that we could do or become (Eph. 2:8-9). You see, if works alone could save us, then the act of water baptism could be seen as the work that washes away the sins of mankind. Jesus wanted us to be knowledgeable about the purpose of water baptism. It was a public statement in the form of a symbolic act of obedience for what has taken place in the Christian's life.

When we arise out of the water, we are declaring something that John the Baptist could only tell the people about: *salvation!* John gave his life "preparing the way of the Lord" (Mark 1:3). We are to prepare the way now by learning to observe (obey) all things Jesus has taught us in His Word (Matt. 28:20) and to be submissive to His ways.

John the Baptist warned the Pharisees and Sadducees (Matt. 3:7-12) about coming to be water baptized without first bringing the "fruits meet for repentance" (Matt. 3:8). He let them know there is a condition to be met prior to being water baptized. They did not believe in Jesus. Instead they were busy mocking and scheming to get rid of Jesus. Baptism would have only been an outward show for them. It was not a public statement of commitment to follow Jesus, but rather it would have been a public spectacle and mockery of all Jesus stood for! The Lord knows our heart and requires us to have it filled with love only for Him when we are ready to request water baptism.

Commitment Is Two Ways
John 3:16-17; Mark 10:45; John 19:30; Romans 10:9-11; Luke 3:8, 24:49

God the Father gave His only Son for our salvation. He sent Christ to be our ransom—not to condemn us but to *ransom* us. (See John 3:16-17, Mark 10:45.)

Jesus fulfilled His ministry and stated, "It is finished" (John 19:30). Jesus said, "Behold, I send the Promise of My Father upon you" (Luke 24:49). The *Holy Spirit* came to abide with us.

Man must accept Jesus as the Son of God, believe He died for our sins, and believe He rose again (Rom. 10:9-11). Man must request water baptism (a sign of our commitment to Christ) out of obedience to God's Word, bearing the fruits of repentance (Luke 3:8). It is not about whom we are, how great a name our family has, or our political connections. It is all about how helpless we are without Him. It is all about Him!

Submersion (or Immersion) Versus Sprinkling?
Matthew 3:13, 16

We must simply follow John the Baptist and Christ's own examples. They were at the river Jordan (Matt. 3:13), and when John baptized Jesus, "Jesus came up immediately from the water" (Matt. 3:16). In order for Jesus to "come up" from the water, He would have had to have been *in* the water. If the Bible had meant sprinkled with water, it would have said it.

A Summary of Water Baptism
Mark 1:4

John could not be the salvation for the people; he could only prepare the way. He was preparing them for *Christ's* ways, not *man's* ways. John preached a sermon of *remission* and *redemption* of their sins (Mark 1:4).

Water baptism is a *public statement* of a repentant spirit for the redemption of your sins. It means you have committed your life to Christ, just as He committed His life to be a ransom for your sins. It means you believe He died for your sins, that He arose from the dead, and that He resides now at the right hand of God the Father.

Commitment Is Two Ways: The Holy Trinity and Man
John 19:30; Romans 10:9-11

1. God the Father gave His only Son as a ransom for our salvation.
2. Christ fulfilled His ministry and stated, "It is finished" (John 19:30).
3. Jesus said He would send the Promise of His Father upon you, which is the Holy Spirit.
4. You must accept Jesus as the Son of God, believe that He died for your sins, and believe that He arose again from the dead (Rom. 10:9-11).
5. You must request water baptism as a sign of commitment to the Lord.

Mark the day of your own water baptism in your memory as a *big* occasion in your Christian walk! It is a special day between you and the Lord. You have followed His commandment to be water baptized, and you have spoken of your love for Him publicly. How pleased God the Father must be with you for following in an act of love and obedience.

— Chapter 6 —

Holy Communion

Introduction
Jeremiah 29:11; John 3:16-17; Mark 10:45; 1 Timothy 2:6; Matthew 6:10, 26:39

This chapter is about our commitment to Jesus, just as He is committed to us. He loved us *before* we even knew He existed. He had plans for us *before* we knew Him! Jeremiah 29:11 states, "For I know the thoughts that I think toward you, says the Lord, thoughts of peace and not of evil, to give you a future and a hope." How awesome! The love, devotion, and dedication He gave to each of us while diligently mapping out a plan for our lives shows us a picture of both a loving father and friend.

Jesus knew the plan of salvation was His purpose for coming to the earth. He and God the Father planned for the way of salvation. Jesus had to carry out the plan. He determined to be committed to us no matter the cost.

John 3:16-17 states, "For God so loved the world that He gave His only begotten Son that whoever believes in Him should not perish but have everlasting life. For God did not send His Son into the world to condemn the world, but that the world through Him might be saved." Mark 10:45 states, "For even the Son of Man did not come to be served, but to serve, and to give His life a ransom for many."

These Scriptures tell of His love to us. However, John 3:17 is often neglected. It portrays a loving Father who did not send His only Son to condemn the world but instead so the world could be saved from their sins. Recall the story of the kidnapped child and the love of the parent found in chapter 1. The father only wants to hug the child, to have him back safely in his loving arms, and to bring him home. This is exactly what John 3:17 is all about. Jesus is referred to as our "ransom" (Mark 10:45, 1 Tim. 2:6). He, the Father, and the Holy Spirit were committed to bringing their children home together. They planned this from the beginning. There must be a way to set the children free from the bondage they were in. The death and resurrection of Jesus Christ was the only way.

Jesus knew when He sat at the table with His disciples and told them about the Lord's Supper that He would have to bear the cross for us soon. Then, in the garden, He prayed a most agonizing prayer of commitment to God to accomplish the Father's will.

Matthew 26:39 states, "Oh My Father, if it is possible, let this cup pass from Me, nevertheless, not as I will, but as You will." Jesus modeled for us how to pray when the situation is not comfortable. There are situations that require us to follow through even when the way seems hard. There are times in our lives when there is just no turning back! It was His love for us and the Father that kept Him heading toward the cross on Calvary. He loved us; He still does! Remember the Lord's Prayer, "Your will be done" (Matt. 6:10). Jesus not only taught the disciples how to pray, but He also practiced it in His own life!

Holy Communion
Luke 22:15-22

Jesus told His disciples concerning Holy Communion (the Lord's Supper), "With fervent desire I have desired to eat this Passover with you before I suffer, for I say to you, I will no longer eat of it until it is fulfilled in the kingdom of God" (Luke 22:15-16).

The statement, "before I suffer" tells me Jesus already *knew* the plan. He knew He was about to go to the cross of Calvary. He stayed committed to the plan even though it was painful in all senses of the word.

Holy Communion Is for Believers Only
1 Corinthians 10:16-17; 21-24, 11:23-31

First Corinthians 10:16 speaks of "communion of the blood of Christ," and verse 17 speaks of "one bread." Christians are referred to as the "bread" (one body,) but we cannot become the "cup." We cannot save people. We, the body of Christ, can only spread the Word of God; salvation belongs to the pure blood of Christ only.

How often we want to tell people their sins are forgiven. As parents, we would gladly bring our children before the Lord and ask for them to be saved. We present our young ones as babies and dedicate them to the Lord in hopes that they will one day follow the Lord on their own. This is not a salvation for the child. It is a dedication by the parents to serve the Lord and to bring up the child in the presence of the Lord. It is not salvation; it is a public statement of commitment.

First Corinthians 10:21 states, "You cannot drink the cup of the Lord and the cup of demons." You must choose the way in which you will live, and the cup is the reminder that you cannot have it both ways; the price was simply too high to be shared. Think about it: you cannot be *free* and be *kidnapped* all at the same time. You are either free or you are in bondage.

First Corinthians 11:29 states, "For he who eats and drinks in an unworthy manner eats and drinks judgment to himself, not discerning the Lord's body." Verse 31 says, "For if we would judge ourselves, we would not be judged." These Scriptures teach us a person cannot be a Christian on Sunday and a sinner on Monday. *We must choose this day . . .* How sad it must be for God the Father to see us refuse to open the door for Christ to enter our lives. He gave His Son for us. He stands at the door and knocks. He paid the ransom for each of us to be free.

What holds us back? We have sinned too much! We are too bad! We cannot be loved by anyone! We do not deserve to be free! Over the years of serving as a prayer partner at church altars, I have heard these statements come out of sincere people's mouths, but they are so *wrong*! Remember, the Father did not come to condemn the world but to set it free! (See John 3:17.) He does not stop to remind us of our past. He has plans to bless us, and we must start living in Him to receive all He has for us.

Christ gave us the example of the Lord's Supper (Holy Communion) and told us to remember Him each time we took it. He did not set a particular date or time to observe communion. However, He did give us one specification to follow each time. We are to *remember* Him and what He did for us that day on the cross. In addition, He gave us a timeline for observing it. He stated we are to observe it until He returns.

Also, since Holy Communion is for remembrance and celebration, it is for the saints of God only. It is for those who have been washed in the blood of the Lamb. It is not for the unbeliever; that would serve only to mock Him.

Looking Back and Looking Forward
1 Corinthians 11:26

First Corinthians 11:26 states, "For as often as you eat this bread and drink this cup, you proclaim the Lord's death till He comes." This Scripture is difficult to understand. Christ was saying to the disciples that not only would He die, but He will return too! That is mind boggling to comprehend. I am so glad He did not stop with the cross; He said He is coming back! I am looking forward to His return! When you take the Lord's Supper, do not forget to end your prayer by rejoicing over His soon return. (For more on His return, refer to my chapter on the rapture.)

Recap
Matthew 26:39

He Knew: Jesus knew the plan of salvation, and still He came to this earth. The plan meant Him giving up His own life for us.

We Know: We are given the plan of salvation as stated in the Word of God.

He Planned: He, the Father, and the Holy Spirit set a plan into action on our behalf.

We Plan: Water baptism is a planned event and is most often scheduled between the believer and the baptizer (normally a pastor).

He Committed: Even in the garden, He prayed, "Not as I will, but as You will" (Matt. 26:39).

We Commit: We are stating through the taking of Holy Communion that we are committed to serving Jesus as Lord and Savior all the days of our life. We are committed to live out His will all our days.

— Chapter 7 —

Baptism in the Holy Spirit

Introduction
Luke 24:45, 49, 51; Acts 1:4-5, 2:39

The baptism in the Holy Spirit was a totally new experience for the followers of Christ, and Jesus knew that if the people were going to be able to comprehend what He was about to command them to do, then He had to first open their understanding so they could comprehend what the Scriptures had already told them. You will read in Luke 24:45 that Jesus "opened their understanding that they might comprehend the Scriptures." He did this for His followers just prior to His ascension to the right hand of the Father. He told them, "Behold, I send the Promise of My Father upon you; but tarry until you are endued with power from on high" (Luke 24:49). Then He led the people out a little farther, lifted up His hands, and blessed them. As Jesus blessed them, He was carried up into heaven. (See Luke 24:51.)

The book of Acts (which was also written by Luke) picks up where the last chapter of Luke left off. However, this time when he is writing of the words Jesus spoke to them just before He ascended on high, he writes, "And being assembled together with them, He *commanded* them not to depart from Jerusalem, but to wait for the Promise of the Father, which, He said, 'you have heard from Me. For John truly baptized with water, but you shall be baptized with the Holy Spirit not many days from now'" (Acts 1:4-5). This time Luke refers to the words Jesus spoke to them as a command. He

51

said, "He commanded them not to depart . . ." Being baptized in the Holy Spirit is so powerful and so important in believers' lives that Jesus did not want them to miss it. He wanted them to tarry until they were endued with *power* from on high. Acts 2:39 says, "For the Promise is to you and to your children, and to all who are afar off, as many as the Lord our God will call." According to the Word, that same promise and expectation is for each of us today.

Let's dwell on Luke 24:45 for a while. Think back to what the disciples had just experienced over the period of the last few days, months, or even years. They had witnessed many wonderful miracles performed by Jesus. They had seen angry crowds take Jesus from them and heard the bitterness of the voices as they yelled, "Crucify Him!" They had watched Jesus die a death upon a cross He did not deserve, and they *knew* it! They had watched their Lord, whom they loved, be placed in a tomb. Then they were struggling to deal with the fact that He was risen! They were now talking and eating with Him.

How could this be? He was dead. They knew that He had died and had been sealed in the tomb. How could this be? He was *alive*! He stayed with them for forty days and continued to teach them, but now He was telling them they would need to go and tarry in Jerusalem until they were endued with power from on high. Why did they need that? They had *Jesus*! He was alive; death could not harm Him. Why would they need more? But Jesus knew there was more to come. He was lifted up into the clouds before their eyes and left them standing and worshipping Him.

The disciples were not going to be able to stand with Jesus physically any longer. Now they were beginning to understand that they needed the power for themselves. Jesus had told them to *go and tarry until they were endued with power!* They had gone through so much that their human minds were stretched beyond all possible understanding. Christ knows when we cannot contain what He needs us to know, and He opens our understanding so we can comprehend the Scriptures. The disciples were about to embark upon an experience they had not ever encountered before, not even when Jesus was physically with them. They needed to be able to understand what He had for them, and they needed it *now*. So do we!

Parallel

There is a parallel between water baptism and Holy Spirit baptism that is worthy of note.

Water Baptism

- The believer should be water baptized just as Jesus modeled.
- The candidate for water baptism should be saved.
- The believer asks to be water baptized.
- The believer is baptized by the minister (or other believers).
- The proof (evidence) is that the believer comes out of the water wet.
- Frequently the believer being baptized is seen by many witnesses.

Baptism in the Holy Spirit

- The believer should be baptized in the Holy Spirit, just as Jesus commanded in Luke 24:49.
- The candidate for baptism in the Holy Spirit should be saved prior to requesting to be baptized.
- The believer asks to the baptized in the Holy Spirit.
- The believer is baptized by Jesus Christ.
- The proof (evidence) is that the believer begins to speak in an *unknown tongue.*
- Frequently the believer is seen and heard by many witnesses speaking in his new heavenly language.

Prophecy
Joel 2:29; Acts 2:14-21; Matthew 3:11; John 7:37-39

Here are some of the verses Jesus was referring to when He told the disciples this experience was foretold in the Scriptures. The Scriptures bear witness to the fact that the Holy Spirit would be poured out upon *all* flesh.

Joel 2:29 says, "And also on My menservants and on My maidservants I will pour out My Spirit in those days."

In Acts 2:14-21, Peter, in his first message to the masses after His own infilling of the Holy Spirit, reminded the crowds that Joel had prophesied this experience when he quoted to them from Joel.

In Matthew 3:11, John the Baptist said, "I indeed baptize you with water unto repentance . . . but He shall baptize you with the Holy Ghost, and with fire."

John 7:38-39 says, "He who believes in Me, as the Scripture has said, out of his heart will flow rivers of living water. But this He spoke concerning the Spirit, whom those believing in Him would receive; for the Holy Spirit was not yet given, because Jesus was not yet glorified."

Jesus' Last Words While on Earth
Luke 24:49

Think about it. How important are the last words of someone before they leave? Are they not the words we cling to in our memories for a lifetime? Jesus knew His last words while standing on earth with His disciples had to be important, powerful, and meaningful. He chose the command, "Go and tarry until . . ." to be His last words spoken to the disciples. He wanted His disciples to let this play over and over in their minds. He did not want them to forget it. He knew they would need this sort of tower of strength to guide them into all truths, and they needed to do it out of obedience and love for Him. His final words were a parting gift of love to them! It is the same parting gift of love He has given to every believer since that day over two thousand years ago.

Didn't I Receive the Holy Spirit When I Got Saved?
Psalm 23

Let's continue with the parallel description between water baptism and baptism in the Holy Spirit we spoke of earlier in this chapter. Wasn't salvation required before we could be baptized in water? Yes. Well, it is the same here. You must have the Holy Spirit within you to be eligible to be baptized in the Holy Spirit. The Holy Spirit entered your life upon your confession of Jesus Christ as your personal Savior. After salvation, you were a candidate to be baptized in the Holy Spirit. The outward appearance of being baptized by water is that you are all wet. The outward appearance of the baptism of the Holy Spirit is speaking in other tongues (a heavenly language other than the one you currently know and speak). However, just as you are changed through salvation, you are also changed when you receive the baptism of the Holy Spirit.

The baptism of the Holy Spirit opens up the doors for many manifestations of the gifts of the Spirit that the believer can only partially exercise prior to the infilling of the Holy Spirit. The baptism of the Holy Spirit also enables the believer to be able to pray for needs in either his own life or of the lives of others in ways they cannot put into words. The Spirit will help us to intercede on behalf of others.

The Holy Spirit is a source of power from on high that is like no other. When we feel weak in our own selves, is the time the Lord can come to us through the Holy Spirit and lift us up beyond our own emotions. Psalm 23 says it so well when David wrote, "He makes me to lie down in green pastures" (Ps. 23:1) and "Yea, though I walk through the valley of the shadow of death, I will fear no evil; for You are with me" (Ps. 23:4). The Holy Spirit will not leave you, nor will you be defenseless with the Holy Spirit in your life.

If you recall, water baptism is a public statement that we have committed our lives to the Lord. We have turned away from our old lives of sin and have dedicated ourselves to serving the Lord. We are saying we have died to the old man and have risen in new life to Christ. Since that is the public statement we are making, we must be saved prior to water baptism or the entire act would be a lie. The same is true of the baptism in the Holy Spirit. The Holy Spirit entered our lives upon our confession of Jesus Christ as our Lord and Savior. The Holy Spirit came to dwell within us to guide us into all truths and to point us to Christ, empowering us to live a victorious Christian life.

Why Do We Need the Baptism of the Holy Spirit?
Acts 1:8; John 14:16-17, 26, 16:13-15; Romans 8:14, 26-27; 1 Corinthians 14:22

The baptism of the Holy Spirit is for believers. Christ knew believers would need power to be strong enough to be the witnesses that He needed them (us) to be for Him. The baptism of the Holy Spirit empowers us to be able to live a powerful Christian life, not a defeated Christian life! (For example look at the drastic change in Peter's ministry after the baptism of the Holy Spirit.) He shows us how the Holy Spirit is to be our:

- Source of power (Acts 1:8)
- Comforter (John 14:16-17)
- Teacher and a reminder (John 14:26)
- Revealer of things to come (John 16:13-15)
- Helper to pray more effectively through Him (Rom. 8:26-27)
- Guide (Rom. 8:14)
- Sign for the unbelievers (1 Cor. 14:22)

Think of it this way: If you are on a journey and all the lands are flat and there are no signal lights, stop signs, or roadblocks, and certainly no mountains to climb, you would only need a good running car or maybe even a comfortable bicycle. However, once you begin to have to navigate around mountains, valleys, roadblocks, and all the traffic of life, you need more. You would begin to search for the best vehicle you could purchase to provide you the safest transportation possible.

The Holy Spirit wants to be that supercharged vehicle (person) that will carry you through all the obstacles of life. (There is no comparison I could have picked to provide a quality of comparison to the dear Holy Spirit. He is much too precious to compare to a filthy old car! But in desperation, I have chosen this example.) The Holy Spirit came in at the beginning of our walk with Christ. He was the one who introduced us to Christ. But He wants us to go higher and deeper in our walk with Christ. He can take us there.

Who Am I Speaking to When I Speak in My New Heavenly Language?
1 Corinthians 14:2

You are speaking to God, not man, when you speak in tongues. "For he who speaks in a tongue does not speak to men, but to God, for no one understands him; however, in the Spirit he speaks mysteries" (1 Cor. 14:2).

How Often Should I Pray in the Spirit?
Ephesians 6:12-13

The baptism of the Holy Spirit, with the evidence of speaking in other tongues, should be used in the Christian's life regularly after receiving Him into your life. The Holy Spirit is not to be received and then put on a shelf in our lives, like some sort of trophy or an event to be checked off in our Christian walk. You should welcome the Holy Spirit and all He brings into your life on a daily basis.

If you truly believe the indwelling of the Holy Spirit was given to you to provide more power for your daily life, then why would you not go into your heavenly prayer language on a regular basis? Do you not take vitamins, eat food that is good for you, exercise, etc., for the purpose of keeping your body healthy and strong? Then why not take good care of your spiritual body? Ephesians 6:12-13 tells us, "For we do not wrestle against flesh and blood, but against principalities, against powers, against the rulers of the darkness of this age, against spiritual hosts of wickedness in the heavenly places. Therefore take up the whole armor of God, that you may be able to withstand in the evil day, and having done all, to stand." We must recognize we need the Holy Spirit to complete the armor of God. We need the fullness of the Godhead. We need to be strengthened daily. Who can tell what a day will bring?

How Important Are Tongues?

We should never seek the infilling of the baptism of the Holy Spirit because we desire to speak in another language. You do not get water baptized because you desire to get wet. No, we were water baptized to follow the example of our Lord. We were making a public statement of our new birth in Jesus Christ and telling all those around us that we intended to serve Jesus as our Lord and Savior.

Well, in like manner, we seek the infilling of the baptism of the Holy Spirit not for the tongues but for the power that will surely come from our new and deeper walk with the Lord. We will be endued with power from on high. If that were not enough, we seek the baptism of the Holy Spirit because it is a gift from the Lord and He told us He would send us another *Helper*. We need help to live our Christian walk. Speaking in *other tongues* is simply the evidence you are in fact filled with the baptism of the Holy Spirit. It is not a subject about which to boast. Do we go around bragging that we speak in our native tongue? No. We might brag that we speak in more than one language, but there is an expectation from our parents that we at least speak in the tongue of our parents. Jesus has the same expectation of us. He wants us to be filled with the language He will give to us individually as His children.

Read 1 Corinthians 12:1-11 for the Spiritual Gifts
1 Corinthians 12:11, 13, 18, 14:5; Ephesians 5:18

God has baptized us all into one Spirit. Therefore, there is one and the same Spirit at salvation and at the baptism of the Holy Spirit (1 Cor. 12:13). God has set the members (body of Christ) as He pleased (1 Cor. 12:18). God has also appointed in the church varieties of tongues (1 Cor. 12:18).

You will find the Holy Spirit has many forms that are beneficial to the Christian body. These manifestations of the Spirit are distributed to each one as He wills (1 Cor. 12:11). They are to benefit and build up the Christian body. Although this chapter was written primarily to teach on the baptism of the Holy Spirit with the evidence of speaking in other tongues, it should be noted that there are manifestations of gifts of the Spirit that become open to the believer once he is baptized in the Spirit. The gift of *other tongues and interpretations* is one. It should not be confused with the baptism of the Holy Spirit. The gifts are distributed to believers as God sees fit for the well being of the body of Christ. But to be used by the Lord for a message to be given out to the people using in an unknown tongue, the believer must first have already received his own prayer language (infilling of the baptism of the Holy Spirit).

The baptism of the Holy Spirit is used in your personal prayer life. There are exceptions, and one is in the use of the gift of *tongues*. Even then there should be someone present who is willing to give out the message to the people. Sometimes the one who gives the message in tongues will also give the interpretation for the people. Paul declares all the gifts are important, but love is the most important. He tells us the proper use of the baptism of the Holy Spirit within the body of Christ: "I wish you all spoke with tongues, but even more that you prophesied: for he who prophecies is greater than he who speaks with tongues, unless indeed he interprets" (1 Cor. 14:5).

Paul understood that although he himself spoke often in tongues, unless others could understand the words, communication would not happen. The Bible declares that hearing comes by the Word of the Lord. Others must be able to understand us to receive the Word. Therefore, the new prayer language you receive is not the one that you would use to teach a Sunday school class; no one would understand you. But it is the language of prayer, so use your new prayer language often when you are in prayer. After all, He gave you this language (tongues) to communicate with Him. Please remember the admonition of Paul when he stated, "And be . . . filled with the Spirit" (Eph. 5:18).

‿ᔇ *Chapter 8* ᔏ‿

Tithes and Offerings

Introduction

This chapter was written to teach and encourage believers that tithes are still a part of the New Testament, and they certainly should be an integral part of believers' lives. Giving must come from obedience to God's Word, a cheerful spirit, and love for the Lord. You will receive so much more than you can ever give to the Lord in return for your faithfulness and obedience to God's Word. Let's learn together how God attached both a blessing and a curse to the act of giving. I want to be on the side of the blessing!

Seek First the Kingdom of God
Malachi 3:10; Matthew 6:33-34, 14:13-21, 17:24-27
(Refer to the activity at the end of this chapter.)

God is a jealous God in that He wants no other people or things to come before our love and devotion to Him. Therefore, He gave us a promise that if we would seek Him with our whole heart above and beyond all other things or people in our lives, He would provide for all our needs. Seeking Him first includes tithing our *first* fruits.

The Lord wants you to place Him first in everything you both do and possess. The Lord does not need tithing to further His Kingdom. He has the power to have the fish bring the monies needed to the shore (Matt. 17:24-27). He has the power to feed five thousand with five loaves and two fish and still have baskets of food left over (Matt. 14:13-21). Tithing is not for His sake but for our sake. We need to tithe. It brings a blessing like no other commandment provides. God stated He would pour out from the windows of heaven blessings that you could not contain if you would trust and obey Him. He has even dared you to try Him! He said, "Try me now in this" (Mal. 3:10).

Matthew 6:33-34 says, "But seek first the kingdom of God and His righteousness, and all these things shall be added unto you. Therefore, do not worry about tomorrow, for tomorrow will worry about its own things. Sufficient for the day is its own trouble." Jesus tells you that if you will truly seek Him first in your life, He will take care of all your needs. We are not to worry about the things of tomorrow. He says we will have enough to deal with in a single day, so put your trust in Him. Seek Him to take care of your needs.

Peter knew they had no money, but Jesus told him they would pay the temple taxes so they would not offend the people where they were staying. Money was never an issue with the Lord. He simply instructed Peter, "Go to the sea, cast in a hook, and take the fish that comes up first. And, when you have opened its mouth, you will find a piece of money; take that and give it to them for Me and you" (Matt. 17:27).

Matthew 14:17-18 says, "And they said to Him, 'We have here only five loaves and two fish.' He said, 'Bring them here to Me.'" If we give what we have to Him, Jesus will take our little and turn it into an amount that not only meets our needs, but He is so merciful that He often leaves handfuls on purpose over and above just for us. Matthew 17:20 says, "So they all ate and were filled, and they took up twelve baskets full of the fragments that remained."

Jesus knows our needs before we ask of Him. In Isaiah 65:24, Jesus said, "It shall come to pass that before they call, I will answer; and while they are still speaking I will hear." He wants us to seek Him first in our lives. Then we will be able to listen to Him as He guides us through our daily walk of life. He will not let us down in any area of our lives. He has so often already sent the answer to our problems long before we ever knew we even had a need! Although He already knows our needs, He wants us to bring to Him our needs out of a spirit of trust, faith, and love.

Tithes Are Only a Portion of Our Responsibilities
Matthew 23:23; Hebrews 11:1

As Jesus was speaking to the multitudes and to His disciples, He stated, "Woe to you, scribes and Pharisees, hypocrites! For you pay tithe of mint and anise and cumin, and have neglected the weightier matters of the law—justice and mercy and faith. These you ought to have done, without leaving the others undone" (Matt. 23:23).

In Matthew, Jesus proves that tithes belong in the New Testament as well as in the Old Testament. "These you ought to have done, without leaving the others undone," tells me Jesus expects us to pay tithes, but there is much more that He also expects of us. He adds that we are not just to pay tithes and be proud of ourselves. We also need to understand tithing is such a basic principle for believers to follow that Christ does not even consider it a big deal. He says the "weightier matters of the law" are *justice, mercy, and faith*. We are to tithe, but we must not forget God wants us to give *justice*, have *mercy*, and practice our *faith* for the benefit of others. He is once again reminding us this is not an "all about *me*" journey. It is a faith walk with the Lord, and we are to look, talk, react, and serve just like Him.

Christ shows justice in a way that man does not define it. Justice is a word that describes a since of balance of the law, but there was no balance of the law when it came to our sins. Jesus took them all for us to the cross at Calvary. He died to give us freedom. He is certainly the model for the word *justice* as He would want us to define it. I have heard justice expressed as "just as if I had never sinned." Jesus takes our words and changes their meanings just as He changes the meanings of our lives. He wants us to show His kind of justice, not man's justice. It will literally change your life when you begin to practice His kind of justice.

Christ modeled mercy upon the cross. He does not want us to forget to apply it to all the people we come in contact with on a daily basis. It is so easy to get caught up in the daily business of keeping records. We say we owe such and such and others owe us, but it does not appear as though these are the records Christ wants us to be most interested in.

According to Hebrews 11:1, "Now faith is the substance of things hoped for, the evidence of things not seen." If you exercise faith in Jesus and put Him first in all your ways, then you will believe and trust Him to supply all your needs. And when you have faith in Jesus, you will also be much more likely to exercise justice and mercy in the truest sense of the words.

Jesus carried the matter of tithes into the New Testament and told the multitudes, "These you ought to have done, without leaving the other's undone" (Matt. 23:23). He still expects us to tithe, but it is such a basic expectation that He does not play it up. It is sort of like telling a doctor he is supposed to try to help the sick. We should not feel we have to tell a doctor to take care of the sick; that is just a basic expectation! But we might remind the doctor once in a while that a good bedside manner, reasonable prices, etc., are important for the people as well as saving their lives. Christ did not seem to think it was necessary to remind people there was a basic expectation for paying tithes, but He did remind them to remember other aspects of their Christian journey.

Tithes—10 Percent Off the Top
Malachi 3:7-11

Malachi 3:7 says, "Yet from the days of your fathers you have gone away from My ordinances and have not kept them. Return to Me, and I will return to you,' says the Lord of hosts. But you said, 'In what way shall we return?'" Jesus was telling the people they had gone away from His ordinances and had not kept them. *From the days of your fathers* indicates to me that as children growing up, this generation was not accustomed to the principle of tithing in their own homes. It sounds like they did not learn the truth and value of tithing and the proper way to give to the Lord. No wonder they were not tithing! But God still held each one accountable and called them *robbers* because they had not tithed as they should have done.

The Lord knew this habit of obedience had not been established in them. He laid the blame on their fathers, so He took the time to reteach this generation about the principle of tithing and how He would provide and even bless them if they would begin to tithe. Every generation is responsible for tithes and offerings, but Jesus takes the time to explain to our generation why it is important and necessary for us to obey this command.

Jesus referred to the storehouse as His house. This leads me to think He was referring to the church. Thus, we are to bring *all* our tithes to the church. I believe we are to bring the tithes to the church where we are spiritually fed—the place where we attend church.

"'And try Me now in this,' says the Lord of hosts, 'If I will not open for you the windows of heaven and pour out for you such blessing that there will not be room enough to receive it'" (Mal. 3:10). This just might be the only dare in the Bible that God gives to the people. Have you ever asked yourself what would be such a blessing that you could not contain it? The banks are certainly willing to hold all the money you could ever receive. Therefore, money cannot be the ultimate blessing of obedience. How about health? I will do my best to contain all the health I can get. His blessings come in many and varied ways. They are given when we need them the most. Finances and health are just small portions of the true blessings of the Lord. Finances and health are just small portions of the true blessings of the Lord. I believe His true blessings are found in the fruit of the Spirit, which I will discuss later in this chapter.

Examples of Tithing and Obstacles

I will use three examples of tithing to demonstrate obedience and the possible obstacles that will arise when one begins to tithe. First, let us look at a parent who gives a young child $10 weekly for an allowance. Perhaps the child does household chores or something to earn his allowance. The parent should begin teaching the child how to be obedient to the Word in the principle of tithing. The parent should explain the principle of the 10 percent and show the child he owes $1 out of his $10 to the Lord. The child is beginning to learn obedience to the tithing principle in his young life.

It should be noted that the child still has all his needs met by the parent. He still lives in his father's home and sits at his father's table every day. He has no needs that his father would not willingly meet for him. Even though the child now has only $9 left after paying his tithes, if the child really needed something and was not able to provide it for himself, his father would immediately try to meet his need out of love for the child.

Next, let us imagine the child has now grown into a young man who has decided it is time to move out and be on his own. He has found a job that pays $1,000 per month. He now has obligations he must meet. In order to pay tithes, he must be obedient, and as he submits his finances before the Lord, he will most likely learn to trust God to meet all his needs. Often, we do not have large savings accounts and unlimited income sources when our own monthly income is small, and therefore we are conscious of our every penny spent. However, because the young man was taught the principle of tithing as a young child, he will tithe a tenth of his gross income, $100, to the Lord. In addition to obedience, the young man is learning to trust the Lord. He might even be a little more able to understand a walk of faith in the Lord for some of his needs.

Now the young man has grown up and is a father with a good-paying job, possibly as a manager of a business. He now earns $10,000 each month. The adult is most likely used to giving directions to others throughout the week. He may have children who want to go to college, several cars sitting in the driveway (one for each child), etc. In other words, he may have debts that equal closely to his monthly income. Hopefully he will have a savings account, mutual funds, etc. that he has prudently accumulated over the years.

In this case, the adult sometimes has to deal with another spiritual battle when he tithes his $1,000 monthly to the church. Since he is used to directing and watching over the needs of others, he may begin to try to tell the pastor (or other members of the church) how and where to spend his tithes. Or he may begin to question why the church would need so much money! After all, there may be many wealthy families in the church who are also tithing. Just how much money do you need to give to the pastor anyway! Then a spirit of greed and/or rebellion can enter the adult, and he may begin to give grudgingly or he splits his tithes and gives to other missions, etc. But all the while, he needs to simply be obedient to God's Word and bring all the tithes into the storehouse. The same principles the Lord applied to the child's tithing applies to the adult. God is no respecter of persons. Remember, God does not need our money; He needs our obedience.

Think about how difficult it must be to begin tithing as an adult. We do not get to go through step one, giving our one dollar to the Lord under the watchful and supportive eyes of our loving Christian parents. We must jump right in at whatever income we are earning and begin to tithe. That takes a big leap of faith, trust, and obedience. But God will serve as a loving parent and will be mindful of your financial concerns all the while. It is so important to start young with the principle of tithing. God understood the lack of parental teaching/instruction for that generation, and He will understand you just as well if you were not taught to tithe in your home either. However, if you were taught to tithe and have fallen away from the principle, it is never too late to begin again.

Christ wants us to come to Him as a child would come to his parent. Think how often, even after you have left your parents' home, you still walk back into their kitchen, open the refrigerator door and get a soda, sandwich, and whatever you want, and you do not feel a bit guilty! It is your home too because you are the child (although you are now an adult living elsewhere). Your Father loves to see you walk right into His spiritual kitchen and act as if you live there! It brings Him pleasure to see you come into His presence and get what you need from Him. Just as the child who learned to tithe, you are still able to go to the Father to have all your needs met. We are all His children, and no matter our age or how much we pay in tithes, it is all a small amount to the Lord. He simply wants us to feel comfortable to come to Him with our needs and to enjoy the bounty He has stored up for us. His "storehouse" never goes empty. He has a vast supply, and He told us if we would, "Bring all the tithes into the storehouse" (Mal. 3:10), He would "pour out for you such a blessing that there will not be room enough to receive it" (Mal. 3:10). He does not lie, and He does not change. He said it, and I believe it.

He Called Them Robbers!
Are You Under a Curse or a Blessing?
Malachi 3:8-12; Galatians 5:22-23

Malachi 3:8 says, "Will a man rob God? Yet you have robbed me! But you say, 'In what way have we robbed you?' In tithes and offerings." God referred to the people who had not paid their tithes to the Lord as *robbers*! He cannot place a blessing upon a robber. A robber is known to be one who steals. He keeps something that does not belong to him. A title of *robber* is one I would never want placed upon me, yet He places it upon every person who does not pay their tithes into the storehouse of God. After this harsh title, He begins to teach people how to erase the title from their names. In fact, He told them that if they would begin to tithe He would, "Rebuke the devourer for your sakes, so that he will not destroy the fruit of your ground, nor shall the vine fail to bear fruit for you in the field, . . . And all nations will call you blessed, for you will be a delightful land" (Mal. 3:11-12).

When God refers to rebuking the devourer so that He would not destroy the fruit of your ground, I believe He is referring to the fruit of the Spirit, "But the fruit of the Spirit is love, joy, peace, longsuffering, kindness, goodness, faithfulness, gentleness, self-control. Against such there is no law" (Galatians 5:22-23). And when He mentions "fruit of your ground," I believe He is referring to the fruit of the Spirit upon your own place of dwelling. Have you ever wondered why there is so much confusion, bitterness, anger, yelling, sadness, etc., in your home? Let me ask you, do you pay tithes on a regular basis? Are you a cheerful giver unto the Lord? If not, maybe these are some of the root problems within the home, because God said He would rebuke the devourer (Satan) from eating up the fruit on our ground. If you do not have God stopping the devourer, then what is there to stop the spoiling of the fruit of the Spirit within your own home? Can you buy peace? Can you buy joy? Can you buy love? *No!* We can buy a lot of things, but none will turn to peace if God is not in it.

Then God goes on to say, "Nor shall the vine fail to bear fruit for you in the field" (Mal. 3:11). Here I believe He is referring to the fruit that reaches outside of your home. How about your place of business? Are you content there? How about the relatives? Are you in harmony with them? How about your prayers for your lost loved ones? Are you seeing answers to your prayers? The list goes on and on, but one thing is sure: God has the power to answer your prayers if you keep the line of communication open and are obedient to His Word. He says to "prove Him now"!

Finally, "And all nations will call you blessed, for you will be a delightful land" (Mal. 3:12). How awesome for others to speak of us in such terms. I want others to see me as a delight in their eyes. I want to be that light set upon a hill that offers rest and peace to others. I want my home to be a place that seems to call out to others as a place of rest. What do you want your home to be known as by others? God assures you He will make it a "delightful land" if we will only obey His Word.

Bonus for Giving
Proverbs 3:9-10; Acts 2:13

"Honor the Lord with your possessions and with the first fruits of all your increase; so your barns will be filled with plenty, and your vats will over flow with new wine" (Prov. 3:9-10). We have discussed how the Lord will rebuke the devourer of your fruit both on your own ground and on the vines in the fields. Now He says He will fill your barns with plenty and your vats will overflow with new wine! Let me address my thoughts on this Scripture. I believe the barns are our homes. He supplies all your needs and leaves handfuls on purpose as He blesses you. Then the vats will over flow with new wine. The New Testament refers to the Holy Spirit as "new wine" in Acts 2:13: "Others mocking said, 'They are full of new wine.'" Jesus will fill us to overflowing with new wine! He will not only take care of our physical needs, such as the daily supplies of the home and family, but He will fill us to overflowing in our spiritual life as well!

Offerings—the Lord Is Watching
Mark 12:43-44; Luke 21:1-4

Mark 12:43-44 says, "So He called His disciples to Himself and said to them, 'Assuredly, I say to you that this poor widow has put in more than all those who have given to the treasury: for they all put in out of their abundance, but she out of her poverty put in all that she had, her whole livelihood.'" The Lord saw that this dear widow had given everything to Him. He only required her to give a tenth, she gave everything! She gave offerings above her tithes even though she was poor! I do not imagine the Lord allowed her to go hungry or without because she had given to Him. No, He had His eye upon her! He was watching over her. How often do we think we cannot tithe because we have no money? But, Jesus' principle of tithes still holds today, and His promises will hold throughout all of eternity. (See also Luke 21:1-4.)

The Lord Loves a Cheerful Giver
2 Corinthians 9:6-15; Haggai 2:8

"But this I say: He who sows sparingly will also reap sparingly, and he who sows bountifully will also reap bountifully. So let each one give as he purposes in his heart, not grudgingly or of necessity; for God loves a cheerful giver. And God is able to make all grace abound toward you, that you always having all sufficiency in all things may have an abundance for every good work" (2 Cor. 9:6-8).

God loves a cheerful giver, not one who gives because God said to do it! He does not want one who holds so tightly to his money and time that it hurts him to give. Remember, from the start we established God does not need your money; He wants to bless you. You cannot be blessed without first obeying and giving your whole heart and all your possessions to the Lord. After all, it all belongs to Him anyway. "'The silver is Mine, and the gold is

Mine,' says the Lord of hosts" (Haggai 2:8). *Cheerful* giving is an intangible gift that is ours to give! This is something we own. We own the attitude of our heart! Choose to give God your all with a cheerful and grateful heart. It will thrill the heart of God!

Finally
2 Corinthians 9:10

"Now may He who supplies seed to the sower, and bread for food, supply and multiply the seed you have sown and increase the fruits of your righteousness" (2 Cor. 9:10). According to this Scripture, Jesus supplies the seed! We do not own anything on our own; all can be given or lost in a single heartbeat. Once we recognize everything belongs to God anyway, it becomes easier to rest in His Word and trust Him for all our needs. But when we sow the seed Jesus has supplied to us, He promises to multiply it. When you give of your offerings, you are giving seed money for the Lord to bless. He has already blessed the tithes portion of your giving by rebuking the devourer so the seed can grow. When you go beyond the tithes, you are bringing about an additional blessing of multiplication from the Lord! You see, He clearly stated He, not you, would multiply the seed. But in addition to multiplication, He said He would *increase the fruits of your righteousness*. As you release your offerings of money, time, or whatever talent you possess, you will find growth in your spiritual life as well.

Follow-Up Activity

On an index card, write out your answers to the following questions:

1. List your loved ones you care about—those who consume a lot of either your time or your thoughts throughout each day.
2. List your career or hobby that seems to fill up your day.
3. List your favorite possessions. This could be anything, like your tractor, car, CDs, boat, money, etc.

Now ask yourself if any of the above lists included Jesus. It is so easy to get caught up within a day and realize at the close of the day that Jesus was left completely out of our thinking. We have careers, hobbies, loved ones to care for, possessions to attend to—the list is endless. However, where do we fit Jesus into all of this? How does He fit into our daily lives?

These are food-for-thought questions that will help us to understand how easy it is to leave Jesus out of our lives. Tithes and offerings are more than money. He wants all of us. He does not want the part that is left over when we finish with our day. That is not *first fruits*. He wants our thoughts to be upon Him when we are fresh. Seek Him early, and let the meditations of your heart be upon Him with your whole heart.

~⚬ Chapter 9 ⚬~

The Christian's Responsibilities

Introduction
Mark 12:29-31; Matthew 28:19-20

As a Christian, what is your responsibility to the Lord? His gift of salvation did not cost you a penny, so how can you give back to God? He asks only that you obey His Word. In this chapter, we will see what God has asked of us as believers.

In Mark 12:29-31, Jesus explains what the first two commandments are for believers of the New-Testament era. As we will see in this chapter, Jesus folds the Ten Commandments into two commandments. He did not do away with the commandments; He completed them through love.

Christ also wants us to be obedient to His Word in our service to Him. Matthew 28:19-20 says, "Go therefore and make disciples of all the nations, baptizing them in the name of the Father and of the Son and of the Holy Spirit, teaching them to observe all things that I have commanded you; and lo, I am with you always, even to the end of the age. Amen." Jesus directs Christians to go out into the world teaching others about Him. Remember the first two commandments of the New Testament? This is the first thing we are to teach people: love for the Lord and for one another.

Jesus' New-Testament commandments do not start with "Thou shall not . . ." No, instead they start with listening to the Lord, loving the Lord, and loving your neighbor as yourself (Mark 12:29). These are totally and radically new concepts that were being taught by the Lord during His time on earth. I contend it is just as radical a concept in today's time as well. We want to justify ourselves, condemn others, and tell others how to live their lives. It is the old, sinful man that tries to creep back into our new spiritual life, and we must keep that in check to live the lives Jesus wants us to have.

Finally, we are to search out our role within the body of Christ, the church. The Lord has work for everyone, and we are to be attentive to His calling upon our lives for service to Him.

Action Words!
Mark 12:29-31; Galatians 5:13-14; Romans 13:8-10; Exodus 20:3-17

A scribe came to Jesus and asked Him which was the first (or most important) commandment. Jesus responded to his question with two new commandments. These commandments exemplify the new covenant so beautifully. They are filled with love and grace. He simply told him to first listen to the Lord and love the Lord with his whole being. The next commandment was to love his neighbor as himself. How simple can it be? But wait! Jesus introduced into the New Testament a way of life for the believers. These are critical commandments to follow if one desires to have a victorious walk with the Lord.

The Lord
Mark 12:29-30

"Jesus answered him, 'The first of all the commandments is: 'Hear O Israel, the Lord our God, the Lord is one. And you shall love the Lord your God with all your heart, with all your soul, with all your mind, and with all your strength,' This is the first commandment" (Mark 12:29-30). Please note that we so often overlook verse 29. It is a critical verse to help us fulfill the first commandment.

Jesus clearly starts His response with, "The first of all the commandments is: 'Hear O Israel . . .'" We typically begin with verse 30, which teaches us to love the Lord our God with our entire being. This is exactly as we should do; however, we have overlooked the first half of the first commandment: *hear the Lord!* How do we hear the Lord? We read His Word daily and listen as He speaks to our hearts through the Spirit, which reveals the intent of His Word for our lives. We also do not do all the talking when we pray; we must listen too.

The key word is *hear!* When we hear the Lord, we begin to understand His heart, His thinking, and His feelings, and we cannot help but fall in love with Him. We first hear the Lord and then the next verse starts with an "and," which connects verses 29 and 30 in Mark 12. The Lord refers to these two Scriptures as *"this is the first commandment,"* but He makes it easy to fall in love with Him; just listen to Him. As you hear Him, you will begin to hear Him sing a love song to you. He loves you! How could you not love Him? He *is* love!

Our Neighbor
Mark 12:29-34; Galatians 5:13-14; Romans 13:8-10; Ex. 20:3-17

Mark 12:29-30 sets the stage for you to be able to fulfill the second commandment, which is stated in verse 31. First you will love the Lord your God with all that is within you by getting to know Him—by *listening* to Him. Then you can love others as He loves you. He tells you, "And the second, like it, is this: 'You shall love your neighbor as yourself.' There is no other commandment greater than these" (Mark 12:31). You can only love your neighbor as yourself *if* you accept the love of Christ toward you first. Does this mean the love you have for others can never go any higher than the love you have for yourself? (Take this question as food for thought in your own life.)

As you commune with Christ and listen to His Word, you will begin to see just how much He loves everyone. Sinners and saints—He loves them all. Now if you are to love your neighbor as yourself, then you must first start with the realization that Christ has totally forgiven you. He holds no grudges! He does not remind you of your faults. He does not nitpick at you day in and day out. He does lift you up with words of encouragement. He does guide you in love, and He does show love and kindness to you at all times. He first starts with showing you how He loves you. He wants you to do the same for your neighbors.

Jesus clearly understood what the scribe was asking when he inquired of Jesus which was the first commandment. Jesus, being Jesus, went a step further and gave the scribe the second commandment as well! However, the scribe was most likely thinking Jesus would choose from among one of the Ten Commandments, which was the young man's law as he knew it. Then he would have an open door to pick an argument with Jesus. No matter which one Jesus selected, the scribe was probably ready to ask why one of the other Ten Commandments would not have been chosen first. But Jesus effectively rolled all of the Ten Commandments into the new two commandments He gave the scribe on that day.

Jesus gave him two new commandments that beautifully summed up the ten. When you look at the original Ten Commandments (see Ex. 20:3-17), you will see how each one can be fit into the two commandments Christ gave us in the New Testament. Now the scribe was left with nothing but praise to the Lord, for what could the scribe possibly add to Jesus' response (Mark 12:32-34)?

Note how neatly the Old Testament commandments fit into the New Testament commandments. Exodus 20:3 says, "You shall have no other gods before Me." Exodus 20:4 says, "You shall not make for yourself a carved image." Exodus 20:7 says, "You shall not take the name of the Lord your God in vain." Exodus 20:8 says, "Remember the Sabbath Day to keep it holy." These are all summed up into the New Testament first commandment, "And you shall love the Lord your God with all your heart, with all your soul, with all your mind, and with all your strength" (Mark 12:30).

Now let us see how neatly the next six commandments fit into the New Testament second commandment. Exodus 20:12 says, "Honor your father and your mother." Exodus 20:13 says, "Thou shall not murder." Exodus 20:14 says, "You shall not commit adultery." Exodus 20:15 says, "You shall not steal." Exodus 20:16 says, "You shall not bear false witness against your neighbor." Exodus 20:17 says, "You shall not covet your neighbor's house." These are all rolled into the New-Testament second commandment, "And the second, like it, is this: 'You shall love your neighbor as yourself.' There is no other commandment greater than these" (Mark 12:31).

Jesus knew when you love God above all others, you will not have to worry about the commandments. They will be observed naturally through a heart of love for God and others.

One Another
John 15:12, 17; 1 Corinthians 13:4-7; Galatians 5:14; Ephesians 4:31-32; Romans 12:9-21

John 15:12 says, "This is My commandment, that you love one another as I have loved you." As you study 1 Corinthians 13:4-7, you will learn how He loves you. Then, once you understand how He loves us, you will be better able to love one another as He has loved us.

How to Love According to Christ
1 Corinthians 13:4-7; 1 John 4:7-8; John 14:6; Hebrews 11:1; Galatians 6:2; Romans 12:9-21; Matthew 7:1; Genesis 1:27

Jesus provided us with what we now refer to as "The Love Chapter" of the Bible in 1 Corinthians 13 to guide our behavior as we grow in love toward one another. In so doing, we see how He loves us.

> Love suffers long and is kind; love does not envy; love does not parade itself, is not puffed up; does not behave rudely, does not seek its own, is not provoked, thinks no evil; does not rejoice in iniquity, but rejoices in the truth; bears all things, believes all things, hopes all things, endures all things (1 Cor. 13:4-7).

Let us take a few minutes to examine each of these phrases. They have a great deal of value since they basically describe God Himself. If you want to see the character of God, look at the love chapter. God is *love!* "Beloved, let us love one another, for love is of God; and everyone who loves is born of God and knows God. He who does not love does not know God, for God is love" (1 John 4:7-8).

Suffers Long and Is Kind

Love suffers long and is kind. This is another one of those connections we frequently overlook. I have often heard that love suffers long. I have even heard that love is kind. Rarely have I heard it taught, however, that love suffers long *and* is kind! You see, it is one thing to go around with a spirit of long suffering, but it paints an entirely different picture to say, "and is kind." How often have we made ourselves suffer for someone out of a Christian spirit of love (or so we thought)? We might even have done a service for the umpteenth time for someone, but did we grumble about it? We may have fussed about our long suffering for someone. Are we showing love if we are long suffering without kindness? I think not.

Jesus clearly added the connector word "and" in this phrase. He wants us to maintain a spirit of kindness when we suffer long with people, just as He does with us. He certainly has a right to grumble and complain about us, but He doesn't. He expects that same spirit of love to be seen within our lives today.

Long suffering—I wonder exactly what that phrase means. It could mean that we have *tolerated* a person who is not behaving in the way we think he or she should. Or it may mean that we have endured someone's non-Christlike behavior toward us without retaliating back in the same fashion he or she did to us. Once again, no matter what our definition of long suffering is, it must be done in kindness.

Does Not Envy

Are we always happy for others' good fortune, or do we wish we were the blessed one instead of them? Why did he get that? I thought I was going to get that promotion, etc.? How easy it is for envy to creep into our spirits. It is often subtle, and we are rarely aware of how deeply rooted within us jealousy is until we hear ourselves speak it aloud. Once given voice, jealousy makes such ugly noise.

Does Not Parade Itself

This is the classic "look at me" syndrome! How great I *am*! Do any of these phrases sound all too familiar: Have you seen what I just did or did you hear about my last award? Did we ever once hear Jesus bragging about a single miracle He performed? No! He went on to the next miracle. He traveled to the next dusty town to preach, heal, and bring life. He was not about promoting Himself; He was about promoting God the Father. We are to do no less. It is good to be thankful and rejoice in our own successes, but be careful that it does not overtake your sense of worth. We are not worth anything without Him. He is so much greater than all that we have done or ever will do that it really puts our bragging into a new perspective.

Is Not Puffed Up

Another word that comes to my mind in this case is pride or being full of oneself! Who wants to be around a person like that very long? How can we be witnesses when our lives are filled with ourselves? How can we possibly be about the Father's business of feeding His sheep when we are stuck on ourselves? Be very careful to guard your heart against pride; it will rob you of many blessings.

Another version of "puffed up" comes to mind when I think of prideful people who will not accept other people's offers to help them. Sometimes we find ourselves in situations where we need help from our fellow man, but due to our own stubborn pride, we resist their help. Do you think this type of person is allowing Jesus to help him or her? I doubt it. We can become so *spiritually minded* that we forget Jesus still has more to teach us and we have not arrived in our spiritual journey with the Lord. Be careful not to tune others, or Christ, out of your life due to your stubbornness or pride. Besides all that, what if God was trying to teach someone else about the principle of giving? If you refuse someone's gift, you have possibly only set him back in his learning process. Giving and receiving are both principles to be learned.

Does Not Behave Rudely

Sometimes we do not even see our own rudeness. This is a good reason to ask the Lord to help you to judge yourself lest anyone else judge you (Matt. 7:1). He can reveal to us our rudeness, and then it is up to us to ask for forgiveness and return to the true love Christ has desired us to reflect to others. Have you ever bragged about how you "told someone off"? We allow the old man to rise up within us, and soon we find ourselves acting no differently than the sinner. If we do not show love even in situations where things are not going our way, then how can we ever expect to be a witness to the sinner next door, at our workplace, or even within our own home?

Does Not Seek Its Own

How can love seek its own? Do we reach out to others outside of our circle of close friends, or do we seek to be only with those who say nice things to us? Do we try to help the hurting? How about that person who was so rude to you—do you seek to bring God's love to him? It is our many differences in this world that makes us a beautiful people. God has placed us here on this earth with a variety of skin tones, languages, cultures, skills, and talents. We need to appreciate what each one can bring into our own personal life and be willing to share in their lives as well.

Is Not Provoked

How often do we use little phrases like, "They made me mad," "They pushed my button," or "I was born with a temper—just excuse it!" Each of these phrases leaves Christ's love totally out of the picture. We were created in His image and should be daily trying to conform into the person He created us to be (Gen. 1:27). He did not create an angry person. We actually create the angry person ourselves. We sometimes take great pride in how well we have groomed our character of *anger*. This is not anything to be proud of, and it certainly does not have to be the way we choose to live our lives in the future.

Thinks No Evil

Have you ever had thoughts of revenge that were hurtful to another? Have you ever rejoiced at someone else's pain or loss? Have you ever wished the worst for someone? These are areas that will lead us outside of the love of God. We must guard our minds against these harmful thoughts. They do not bring life; they bring pain and death to those we are thinking them toward and to ourselves.

Does Not Rejoice in Iniquity

Iniquity is just another way of saying a gross injustice has been done to someone. How easy it is to rejoice in unfairness toward someone who has hurt or troubled us! How easy it is to quickly say, "Well, good, they deserved everything they got!" We are not to rejoice in the iniquity of others.

But Rejoices in the Truth

Recall that Jesus is Truth (John 14:6). Go to the Word of God and find the truth for every situation. When you find others appear to be able to live a lie, remember that only Jesus can provide the truth for your life, and He requires us to live as He lived. He was truthful at all times, no matter the cost to Himself. He expects you to live in truth and to rejoice in Him.

Jesus told us, "I am the way, the truth, and the life. No one comes to the Father except through Me" (John 14:6). He is the truth, and we can rejoice in Him.

Bears All Things

Bearing all things leaves little room for us to give up and quit. Not only are we to bear our own things, but we are also to bear "one another's burdens" (Gal. 6:2). Operating under the principle of bearing one another's burdens means once we begin to bear someone else's burdens, then another Christian is also helping us to bear our own burden. It is frequently easier to pray for others and to bear someone else's burden than our own. The Lord knows we need others in this Christian walk, and He has directed us to bear one another's burdens. Thank the Lord!

Believes All Things

We can do this by simply believing that Jesus is the Son of God, that He died for our sins, and that He arose again on the third day. Once you know and believe that Christ is your Savior and that He is truly God, then believing becomes simple. If you can trust Him for your eternal life, why can't you believe Him for the tedious things that come upon you?

Hopes All Things

Hope gives you the opportunity to enter a faith walk with Christ. "Now faith is the substance of things hoped for, the evidence of things not seen" (Heb. 11:1). We do not need to have faith or hope for what we can already hold in our hands; we hope for things we have yet to see. The evidence of a faith walk is that you cannot see what you have trusted the Lord to provide for you. You are trusting in Him. You are hoping in Him, not in yourself. How easy it is to give up too quickly on our faith walk simply because we do not see what we are hoping for. Patience is often not one of my better virtues; how about you? I want it, and I want it right now! I am sorry, but a faith walk is not based upon our timeline; it is God's timeline and they are often two entirely different clocks. Be patient and trust God.

Endures All Things

In our relationship with Christ, does He ever say to us, "I'm not going to help you. You are on your own"? No! Christ said He would never leave us, and therefore He will always endure all things with us. We too must follow His example. We cannot walk away from a situation in our life just because it gets rough. Jesus has given us all the tools we need to see a situation through. The good news, though, is that you never have to endure the situation alone. He will be with you every step of the way, but, He usually wants us to go through the situation by not giving up on it and trusting in Him.

There are times the situations or trials are for our own learning. We do not want to shortchange our learning process that God has allowed us to experience for growth in our faith in Him.

Romans 12:9-21 restates the characteristics of love and tells us, "Let love be without hypocrisy. Abhor what is evil. Cling to what is good" (Rom. 12:9). If we cling to what is good, we cannot possibly be looking for the bad in others at the same time. Therefore, let us look for the good in others at all times.

Go and Make Disciples
Matthew 5:17, 23:23, 28:19-20; Luke 24:49

> Go therefore and make disciples of all the nations, baptizing them in the name of the Father and of the Son and of the Holy Spirit, teaching them to observe all things that I have commanded you; and lo, I am with you always, even to the end of the age. Amen (Matt. 28:19-20).

Note, He *"commanded you"* to love the Lord, your neighbor, and one another! If only we could teach people to love the Lord with all their being and to love one another as themselves! How much more pleasant a world we would live in.

Jesus wants us to teach the believers how to be *disciples*. We are to teach them to "observe all things that I have commanded you." What are the other "things" He has commanded us to do? One that comes to mind is to be obedient with our tithes and offerings (Matt. 23:23). Another is to obey the Ten Commandments, or as we have seen, the first two commandments of the New Testament. Jesus said He did not come into the world to do away with the law but that the law through Him might be perfected (Matt. 5:17).

Jesus also told the disciples to "go and tarry until they were endued with power from on high" (Luke 24:49). There are so many things we need to teach the people to train them to become followers of Him. It will be a lifetime of service unto the Lord just teaching believers about the mighty works of God.

Seek Your Place in God's Kingdom
Romans 12:3-8; 1 Corinthians 3:5-9, 12:27-31; Matthew 28:19-20

A heart of love brings obedience. We want to obey and please the one we love. It just seems to flow in a natural progression when we fall in love with someone; we look for ways to please him or her. We do not search out various ways to please those we love just to hear them brag on us. No, we do it because we want to make them happy and content in their own lives. We do it just because we love them and seek no outward show of approval.

True love can often be given in a one-way direction of affection. Think about it—Jesus gave His love to us while we were yet sinners. He did not wait until after we were already doing great acts of servitude for Him to begin loving us. He loved us first. You must be willing to serve Him even on those rare occasions when you say to yourself you cannot feel a thing spiritually. You need to serve Him because of who He is, not just because you want something in return for your love. To be accepted by the Lord, all your outward acts of obedience must originate in the heart (spirit); otherwise they are simply done for show.

Seek out Your Place within the Body of Christ
Romans 12:3-8; 1 Corinthians 3:5-9, 12:27-31; Matthew 28:19-20

Christ tells us in Romans 12:3-8 that we have many diverse gifts of ministry that are to be used within the body of Christ. First Corinthians 12:27-31 refers to some of the roles of ministry within the body of Christ. The Scriptures clearly point out that we have different roles to be served out in the body.

Jesus wants us to seek out the "best gifts" for our lives. "But earnestly desire the best gifts. And yet I show you a more excellent way" (1 Cor. 12:31). The more excellent way refers to the love of God and the behavior we should model as Christians. Using the characteristics of love, we need to seek out our role within the body of Christ as well as our role outside the body of Christ.

I have written of the fact that Christ wants us to, "Go therefore and make disciples of all the nations, baptizing them in the name of the Father and of the Son and of the Holy Spirit, teaching them to observe all things that I have commanded you; and lo, I am with you always, even to the end of the age. Amen" (Matt. 28:19-20). Seek the Lord for the direction He has planned for you in the area of service for both the body of Christ (the church and fellow believers) and the service He wants to use you in outside of the body of Christ.

Jesus shows us repeatedly in His Word how He sought the lost; we can do no less. We will strive to make disciples (followers of Christ) by using the gifts God has bestowed upon us individually. We are all different. One person may be able to reach someone where another person could not. Some will plant the seed, others will water, and still others will reap the harvest (1 Cor. 3:5-9). We may do all three over the course of time, but nothing will be done without us first seeking the Lord for His divine guidance for our lives.

To help you seek out your role within and without the Body of Christ, try answering the following questions.

Questions

1. What are the talents I believe the Lord has given to me?
2. What are the strong points about my character (personality traits)?
3. I feel most comfortable when I am doing _____ for others. Explain your answer.
4. I feel least comfortable doing:
5. I would like to try performing the following service in the church:

Once you have answered these reflective questions, ask yourself if you are already serving the Lord in a way that aligns to your most comfortable feelings. Are you doing things for the Lord that make you feel miserable? If so, why?

Are you outside of your comfort zone? Moses sure was! He asked the Lord to get someone else for the task at hand. "But Moses said to God, 'Who am I that I should go to Pharaoh, and that I should bring the children of Israel out of Egypt?" (Ex. 3:11). The Lord provided Moses what he needed for the task. Simply being outside of our comfort zones does not always mean this is not the task the Lord has asked us to do. However, it could be. It is certainly worth doing what Moses did. Ask the Lord if this is really the task He wants you to do. Sometimes we begin a good work for the Lord simply because we are caught up in the moment. We do not go to the Lord in prayer about the service first. We say yes before praying. Although it may be a wonderful service, it may not be the one the Lord has designed for you at this time in your life. Always pray for guidance for your service that He has planned for you today.

After seeking your role in the body of Christ, if you are not currently serving the Lord in the capacity God has planned for you, seek counsel from your church's pastor. He will begin to pray with you about fulfilling the call that God has placed upon your life.

∽୨ *Chapter 10* ୧∽

The Christian's Inheritance

Introduction
Revelation 22; John 16:13-15; Acts 1:8; Luke 24:49

We can often find television shows, books, or Internet reports portraying people who just inherited a large sum of money. They may have been totally surprised by their inheritance or they have been waiting to receive it; either way, it was their inheritance. Then there are the reports of those who have been cheated out of an inheritance for various reasons. Ah, then there are those folks who do not receive a penny from their loved ones.

But I have good news! Every Christian is not only going to inherit great wealth, but they will also inherit all the love, health, joy, and peace they could ever desire that will last for an eternity! In addition, they will begin to draw on their inheritance now. God the Father knows how to take care of His children, and when we accept Jesus into our lives, we immediately become a joint heir with Jesus. The Bible talks of the streets of gold, the river of life, the fruit tree that bears twelve different fruits, and the mansions, but that is just the start! The Bible also speaks of the Holy Spirit being sent to this earth to be our guide and our source of power. These attributes of the Holy Spirit are given to you, the believer, now so you can begin to live a victorious Christian life.

In this chapter, we will begin to reflect upon our blessings as we look at some of the many gifts of love we receive while living here on earth. We will also look at the aspect of inheritance from man's version. We will find we have a "witness" to stand by us during any heavenly questioning concerning our right to inherit our heavenly birthright.

First Establish Your Relationship
Romans 8:14-18; Ephesians 1:3-14, 3:6

When you accept Jesus Christ as your personal Savior, the Holy Spirit comes into your life to live with you. Therefore, who better to testify that you are who you say you are than the Holy Spirit? The Bible tells us the Holy Spirit will stand as a witness on your behalf declaring you are in fact a child of the King. "The Spirit Himself bears witness with our spirit that we are children of God" (Rom. 8:16).

In a courtroom, you cannot be your own witness. You need a reliable witness to confirm you are a child of God. This is one of the many blessings you have when you allow the Holy Spirit to enter your life at the time of your salvation. He will always guide you in all truths, and He will always testify only the truth on your behalf. The Bible even refers to the Holy Spirit as our "guarantee" and our "seal." Ephesians 1:13-14 tells us, "In Him you also trusted, after you heard the word of truth, the gospel of your salvation; in whom also having believed, you were sealed with the Holy Spirit of promise, who is the guarantee of our inheritance until the redemption of the purchased possession, to the praise of His glory."

What is the Holy Spirit attesting to on your behalf? He is testifying that you are a child of the King. Hearing "child of the King" can simply sound nice to your ears, but think about what being a child of the King means to you. You are adopted. You *are* His child! Paul tells us in Romans 8:15 that we can refer to God the Father as "Abba, Father," or as I have heard it for many years, "My Father." Abba refers to a relationship that only a child can have with a father. Once you accept Jesus Christ into your heart, you inherit the right to refer to God the Father as "Abba Father." You are no longer an outsider; you are family.

Romans 8:14-17 tells us:

> For as many as are led by the Spirit of God, these are sons of God. For you did not receive the spirit of bondage again to fear, but you received the Spirit of adoption by whom we cry out, "Abba, Father."
>
> The Spirit Himself bears witness with our spirit that we are children of God, and if children, then heirs—heirs of God and joint heirs with Christ, if indeed we suffer with Him, that we may also be glorified together.

Jesus wanted to make sure both the Jews and the Gentiles were included in salvation when He had Paul write, "that the Gentiles should be fellow heirs, of the same body, and partakers of His promise in Christ through the gospel" (Eph. 3:6).

The adoptive parent, God the Father, chose to adopt us before we knew Him. It is not like we were begging and twisting His arm to adopt us. We did not even know Him! He knew us first, and He still wanted us to be His children. Also, in the legal process of adoption, the parent usually gives the child their last name; God the Father, God the Son, and God the Holy Spirit are our new names! Then, because of rightful ownership under the adoptive parent's name, the child is rightful heir to inherit all the parent has left for the child.

Think of a courtroom scene. Your attorney is brilliant at bringing in solid witnesses. In this case, there is only one witness who can stand up for you. He is the Holy Spirit, and He is the "guarantee" (witness or seal) for you. He declares you are the rightful heir to the title of God's child. No one can dispute such an honest witness as the Holy Spirit because He, like the Father and Son, cannot lie!

The Holy Spirit, your seal and promise (Rom. 8:16-17), stands beside you to whisper into your own spirit that this is all real. You are indeed a child of the most high God! But in your excitement over the promise that you are His child, you should not forget the condition that is written into Romans 8:17, "If indeed we suffer with Him that we may also be glorified together." You are to go through your life living as a Christian, a child of the King, and a witness for and of Him. He will do the same for you.

"If indeed we suffer with Him." Does this mean that we have to suffer, as in to experience pain? The Greek word used for "suffer" in Romans is *sympascho*, which interpreted is "to experience pain jointly or of the same kind (specifically persecution; to 'sympathize'):—suffer with."[1] We need to understand that in our Christian walk, we will experience pain—the kind of pain Jesus suffered. The pain He suffered, even more than the pain of the cross, was of a broken heart over a lost and dying world. Yes, there may be times when you suffer persecution for Christ's sake. You may be teased, bullied, disowned as a family member or even a church member, or ridiculed because you are a Christian. But the greatest pain you may ever suffer (share jointly with Christ) is a broken heart over a dying world. Are you ready and willing to share this pain with Him? If you are a believer and have allowed this pain to be dulled in your spirit, begin to ask the Lord to rekindle the pain of a lost and dying world within your spirit.

Recognize You Have a New Last Name
Revelation 2:17, 3:5, 12, 19:12, 13, 16, 22:4; John 10:3, 14:13-14, 20:31

I suppose if I were to ask you, "What is your last name?" you would immediately give me the surname that appears on your birth certificate. That name was recorded in a book of records in the local courthouse. However, there are some people who do not know, or who have lost, their parents, and along with it seemed to go their legal surname and their inheritance.

Let me give you a very personal example of what I'm talking about. My father was an orphan at the age of four. He was kept in an orphanage until the age of nine, and then he was shipped from New York state, where he

---

[1] James Strong, S.T.D, LL.D, *Strong's Exhaustive Concordance of the Bible* (Peabody, Massachusetts: 2007), 1125.

was born, down to Texas. He, along with many others, rode the "Orphanage Train" to Texas. The state of Texas needed workers to help in the fields, and the state of New York had such a large number of orphans that the two states must have seen an opportunity for a win-win situation and somehow made an arrangement to help one another.

Thus, Dad ended up in an orphanage in Texas. He was finally selected by a sweet Christian family to come and live with them. He would help out on the farm, and they would give him a bed, food, and clothing and send him to school. He was probably one of the more fortunate ones! However, they never adopted Dad. He was forever an orphan who was blessed to at least have a kind foster family. They had their last name, and he had his last name; they were not the same. It was obvious to everyone that he was not one of them because their last names were different.

Dad worked faithfully in the fields and grew up under their roof. However, when the foster parents died, he was not listed in the family will. Once the foster parents were gone, he felt as though he had walked away from the home with no more than what he had entered it with many, many years before. Although he was now an adult, Dad once again felt like an orphan and alone! He did all that was asked of him, but he received nothing in the will simply because he was not legally an heir. We cannot assume we are someone's child unless we are legally made a child through birth or adoption. Dad was neither.

Dad's history finally helped me to understand why he could not seem to grasp the love of God. When I was four years old, my dad asked Jesus into his heart. He believed Jesus died for him. Dad tried to be a good Christian, but he just didn't seem to change very much over the years. He continued to be bitter and so easily angered. He suffered with severe headaches and other stress-related types of issues. Then, when I was sixteen years old, my dad walked down to the altar (as he had done before), but this time it was very different. Within days my dad began to drastically change! He became so loving, kind, and gentle, and he laughed a lot too. My dad had found true joy! Dad died seven years later, and his last words to me on the night of his death were, "Tell James (his pastor) not to worry about me because I'm in the palm of His hand." I did not know those were to be Dad's last words, but how profound they were!

It was probably another twenty years after Dad's death before I finally understood why it took Dad so long to come around to a fulfilling relationship with Jesus. The Lord showed me one day that Dad only understood conditional love. He could stay under the roof of his foster parents *if* he worked for them and did as he was told. They would provide his basic needs, and he would be obedient. Let me make it very clear for the record: my Dad had a loving foster family. They treated him with love and respect. I do not know how or when conditional love became the basis for Dad's learning how to survive; my guess is it began as early as age four. But I am quite certain looking back now as an adult that Dad only understood that one form of love.

For at least twelve years my dad was obedient to the Word of God, and he trusted Jesus would give him salvation *if* he did exactly as told. When Dad broke one of the rules in God's Word, he felt bad and frustrated. But one day the Lord must have somehow convinced Dad that he was *adopted*! He had a last name: God the Father, God the Son, and God the Holy Spirit. He was not an orphan who could be tossed out if he slipped up. He was *loved and wanted*. He was given a *name*! My dad became the door-greeter at the church. Why? He belonged there and wanted everyone to feel welcome in the Lord's home—and in his home too. You see, even the church you attend appears different when you understand that this is your house too.

Dad not only had salvation; he had an inheritance! But because of his new name, he also had all the rights and privileges of a child while he lived. He could go and come in freedom and not condemnation. He could ask of his Father anything, and the Father would give it to him, if it were in Dad's best interest. He had a relationship that was real. He was loved and wanted now. He didn't have to wait until his death to have his inheritance. He was able to start drawing upon his inheritance now. What joy my Dad experienced in his last seven years of life.

What Is Your Inheritance?

Heaven is frequently the first thought that comes to mind when we are asked, "What is your inheritance as a Christian?" However, we will learn through God's Word that our inheritance begins way before we enter heaven. Heaven is certainly a correct response, but we have so much more in our spiritual account that is available to us to draw from now.

When you accept Jesus into your life and believe that He is the Son of God and that He died and rose again for your sins, you become a child of God. You are adopted into the family of God. With your adoption, as we have studied, comes a rightful inheritance. Salvation is so often thought of as a freedom from going to hell. Now you are saved and have eternal life in Jesus; you have heaven to go to when you die.

Let us look at what else you have once you become a child of the King. I am certain you will be able to think of many more instances in your own Christian walk with the Lord than just the ones I have listed for you to review.

Relationship
Romans 8:14-17; 1 John 3:2

Romans 8:14-17 states:

> For as many as are led by the Spirit of God, these are sons of God. For you did not receive the spirit of bondage again to fear, but you received the Spirit of adoption by whom we cry out, "Abba, Father." The Spirit Himself bears witness with our spirit that we are children of God, and if children, then heirs—heirs of God and joint heirs with Christ, if indeed we suffer with Him, that we may also be glorified together.

We have such a close relationship with God that it is declared in His Word we are adopted. God has become our *Father*! If you were blessed with a loving and godly father, think of all the times you had with him. How often did you get to climb up onto his lap, play games with him, cry with him, eat with him, share with him, and confide in him? Now understand that God *is* your Father. He desires for you to climb up in His lap, play, cry, eat, share, and confide in Him. He desires to have a close and personal relationship with you, His child.

A Savior
John 3:15-17

God so loved you that He gave His only begotten Son to die in your place. He did not send Jesus to condemn you but to save you. He wants you to be His child. He wants you back. Remember in the Garden of Eden, God walked with man. He wants a relationship with you once again that will be one of communion and sharing.

Love
Ephesians 3:19; 1 John 4:7-8; John 17:23-26

The love of God passes all our understanding. There are so many times when we cannot comprehend how He could possibly love us. We have not done anything worthy of a King's inheritance. Certainly one might ask, "Who am I that a King would have so much love for me that He would be willing to die for me?" His love is pure, perfect, and unconditional. He does not give out with an expectation it be repaid in like manner. However, He does long for your worship. He does desire a broken and contrite spirit. He does enjoy your fellowship. As much as a loving father would desire a relationship from his own child, even greater is the desire of God for a relationship with you.

Likeness
Genesis 1:26; Galatians 5:22-25; Ephesians 3:2; 2 Corinthians 3:18; Philippians 3:21

Genesis 1:26 states, "Then God said, 'Let us make man in Our image, according to Our likeness.'" Second Corinthians 3:18 says, "Are being transformed into the same image from glory to glory, just as by the Spirit of the Lord." You were created in His image, and you are to be transformed daily into the likeness of His image. Remember the fruit of the Spirit (Gal. 5:22-25). As you grow in the fruit of the Spirit, you will begin to resemble your Creator more and more.

Citizenship/Home
Philippians 3:20-21; John 14:1-3

This earthly residence is not your final home. Jesus Christ said He would go and prepare a place for you and that He would return to take you to be with Him in the heavens. Your roots and your treasures should both be placed in heavenly matters; all else will be left behind and will not travel with you. Do you have a longing for your real home?

A Friend
Proverbs 18:24; Acts 3:26

"A man who has friends must himself be friendly, but there is a friend who sticks closer than a brother" (Prov. 18:24). Jesus is closer than our own family members. He is with you at all times. He is the one you can confide your deepest secrets to. He is always faithful to your love for Him, and His thoughts are for your benefit. He desires to bless you, never to harm you. God sent Jesus to bless us! And oh how many times we have been blessed by His presence in our lives. What a friend we have in Jesus!

Gifts and Graces
Romans 12:3-8; 1 Corinthians 12; John 1:16

Jesus gave us gifts to be used while on earth. The gifts are given to the individual as it is needed in a given situation. The believer should remain open to the gifts and be willing to use them as God pours them out. Gifts are given as needed to edify or build up other believers. There are diversities of gifts to be used by the believer as a source of help or guidance for various situations as God allows them to be used. First Corinthians 12:8-11 shows us the various gifts:

For to one is given the word of wisdom through the Spirit, to another the word of knowledge through the same Spirit, to another faith, by the same Spirit, to another gifts of healings by the same Spirit, to another the working of miracles, to another prophecy, to another different kinds of tongues, to another the interpretation of tongues, but one and the same Spirit works all these things, distributing to each one individually as He wills.

Fruit of the Spirit
Galatians 5:22-23

In this world, we find there are times when it is difficult to live a victorious life. We could so easily slip into grumbling and complaining, bitterness, and even hatred! But Jesus knew the world all too well and sent us the fruit of the Spirit to help us walk through these times of tribulation in a graceful manner. "But the fruit of the Spirit is love, joy, peace, longsuffering, kindness, goodness, faithfulness, gentleness, self-control. Against such there is no law" (Gal. 5:22-23). Jesus knew we would need to draw upon the fruit of the Spirit often to be the Christian witness He desired for us to become. Notice the last sentence in verse 23 states, "Against such there is no law." When we do good for one another, or when we experience pure, godly love and joy, we are not breaking any laws. Man does not write laws against kindness; he writes them to protect against harm. We can freely exercise the fruit of the Spirit.

God has given us fruit that is not bound by laws. Think about this: can anyone steal your joy? *No!* You have to give it away. Joy is not tangible. We may have outward appearances that reflect we have joy, but no one can steal it from us. The same is true of peace, kindness, etc. Man cannot steal or write laws that would prohibit us from experiencing the fruit of the Spirit. This fruit is not carnal; it is spiritual. It brings life to us and blessings to those around us. We must strive to grow in the fruit of the Spirit. The more we exercise the use of the fruit, the stronger we become as Christian examples for others. When this happens, nonbelievers are more likely to want to have what we have: our Christian faith.

Do you recall chapter 8 on tithes and offerings? I stated the principle of tithing as God has laid it out for us in Malachi and said He tells us He will rebuke the devourer for our sake. The devourer (Satan) would love to steal and destroy your fruit of the Spirit, but he is held back from robbing you based upon your obedience to tithing. Who would have ever thought your love, joy, or even self-control could be tied to your tithing! If you are struggling in any of these areas, check out your tithing. If you say, "But I am tithing, and I still have no joy or self-control in my life." Then I would have to redirect you to look at your heart and attitude as you give of your tithes and offerings. Are you giving as a cheerful giver or do you simply give out of obedience? God will always honor His Word. Have you honored your part in respect to His Word?

Supply
Isaiah 65:24; Matthew 6:25-34; Philippians 4:19; Romans 8:24-25; Hebrews 11:1

After I married and moved away from home, I recall how often I would return home to my mother's home and walk into the kitchen. I would walk around, find what looked good, and ask if I could have it. Mother always said yes. She even seemed a bit pleased that I wanted things from her kitchen. Mother was a good cook, and there was always something that I wanted when I went to her house. Even though I had already moved out, it still felt like home when I went back to my parents' home. There was just no other feeling quite like it. Going to a friend's home was nice, but it still wasn't home to me.

Jesus is always pleased when His children want to walk around in His kitchen and ask for something good to eat. He offers more than desserts (the desires of our hearts); He also offers steak and potatoes (the Word). How often do you go and just sit in His kitchen? How often do you sit around the table and visit with the Lord? You may think this is not possible, but it is! Take time to sit and read God's Word, pray, and commune with the Lord. You will find that it is just as comfortable as sitting at the table and sharing a cup of coffee with your own father, mother, or best friend.

Jesus said, "It shall come to pass that before they call, I will answer; and while they are still speaking, I will hear" (Isa. 65:24). Jesus wants you to speak to Him about your needs, concerns, and problems; you must recognize, however, that even before you were aware of your troubles, He had already begun working on the solution(s).

You have yesterday's memories, and you have today's situations, but you do *not* have tomorrow until it becomes *today*. Only the Lord has your tomorrows. He is the one who sets in motion the events of tomorrow. You can only work within the moment, not even the hour. Therefore, since Jesus knows what you need for both today and tomorrow, He puts the pieces of your life together to create solutions for your problems while you are just beginning to learn that you even have a problem! He is always way ahead of you! Trust Him. He never sleeps, and He certainly never forgets about you. He cannot lie, and therefore when He says to trust Him, it is really that simple.

How easy it is to get caught up in the cares of this world. We find ourselves fretting and worrying over the smallest of things. Certainly worrying over the big things will not bring an answer any faster. Matthew 6:33-34 says, "But seek first the kingdom of God and His righteousness, and all these things shall be added to you. Therefore do not worry about tomorrow, for tomorrow will worry about its own things. Sufficient for the day is its own trouble."

You have enough to deal with when you operate in the here and now. You do not need to try to fix tomorrow's troubles on today's timetable. Turn tomorrow over to the Lord and He can work on it for you. Remember, He is the only one who has the power to tomorrow's issues today. If we keep ourselves busy seeking Him first, He has promised to take care of all these other things in our lives.

As a child of the King, you have riches that are yet to be counted. Philippians 4:19 states, "And my God shall supply all your need, according to His riches in glory by Christ Jesus." Since our Father owns the entire universe, I believe He is capable of paying next month's rent and utility bills for us. Satan would love for you to forget just how wealthy your heavenly Father really is, and he sure wants you to forget that Jesus loves it when you ask of Him whatever you need. He is capable and able to supply all your needs; just ask Him.

There are times when the Lord wants you to take a trip on a faith walk with Him. In Romans 8:24-25 we find that we do not need to have faith for the things we can clearly see. Why would one need faith for something he is holding tightly to in his own hands? That makes no since. Faith is exercised when we need something we do not have yet. We have a need, and we do not see a human solution (at the time of the request). "For we were saved in this hope, but hope that is seen is not hope; for why does one still hope for what he sees? But if we hope for what we do not see, we eagerly wait for it with perseverance" (Rom. 8:24-25). Christ wants you to exercise the same hope you used to receive your salvation to attain answers in the spiritual world for your needs.

We eagerly wait for it with perseverance is almost like saying "run but wait." The word *eagerly* reminds me of people who are excited in a good sense of the word. They are thrilled about an upcoming event. They just can't wait! But then the Lord said *with perseverance*. Now *with perseverance* sounds to me like I am to not give up hope, but the Lord just told me how I am to wait for my answer: *eagerly*. He also tells me to never give up. Do you get the picture? Faith requires a trust that is so complete in the fullness and awesome power of God that we can look for our answer, no matter the length of the timeline God has designed for us, with an inner excitement and peace.

Hebrews 11:1 defines faith as, "Now faith is the substance of things hoped for, the evidence of things not seen." Just remember that whenever you have a need and take it to the Lord, believing that He is able to deal effectively with your problems, you have just begun a faith walk. The evidence that you are on a faith walk is very simple; you cannot see a thing! You cannot see the answer. You often do not even have a clue how to solve the problem. But God knows how to deal with your problem. He has already started the answer process on your behalf (remember Isa. 65:24). You are to trust and obey; He is to honor His Word. Relax—God's in control.

Health

John 19:30; Matthew 8:17; 1 Peter 2:24; John 10:10; Romans 8:11; Luke 5:17

There are many powerful examples of mighty healings found in the Word of God. But the simple truth is that they are written about other people. Have you ever wanted something that had *your* name on it? Well, healing has your personal name on it, just as salvation does. We read in John 19:30, "So when Jesus had received the sour wine, He said, 'It is finished!' And bowing His head, he gave up His spirit." You see, Jesus did not just purchase your salvation on the cross; He also purchased your healing. *"It is finished!"* is His assurance to us that it is *paid for in full.*

There is nothing you can do to add to what Christ has already done to receive your salvation or your healing. They were purchased with your name on them way back at Calvary. Jesus had you and me in mind when He allowed them to crucify Him on the cross that day. Matthew 8:17 states, "He Himself took our infirmities and bore our sicknesses." And 1 Peter 2:24 says, "Who Himself bore our sins in His own body on the tree, that we having died to sins, might live for righteousness—by whose stripes you were healed." He took upon Himself all our sicknesses and bore all our infirmities so we might have more than salvation and eternal life. You see, He wanted you to have life abundantly even in this life on earth. He cared about you enough to go the extra mile and receive the stripes for your healing. Do not let a single stripe go unused! Whenever you need a healing for your body or your mind, ask Jesus. After all, He has already purchased it with His own body.

Power of Attorney

John 14:13-14

There are times when we need to be given a power of attorney to help someone else. Sometimes we need this sort of power because our loved one is no longer able to care for himself or we need to be able to stand in the gap and speak on his behalf. When we act in this capacity, it is understood that we are always keeping the best interest of the one we are helping at the forefront of our thoughts. All our actions and deeds should be to best serve them.

When my mother was elderly and became very ill, we realized I needed to have a power of attorney over her bank account. I needed to be able to sign on her behalf and to ultimately make decisions for her; always keeping her best interest at the root of all of my decisions. God the Father gave to Jesus all authority and power. Jesus in turn grants to us the authority to ask in His name and He will do it.

"And whatever you ask in My name, that I will do, that the Father may be glorified in the Son. If you ask anything in My name, I will do it" (John 14:13-14). What authority we have been given in the name of the Lord! But with this authority comes responsibility. We must know the heart of the Father to know how to spend His money, His talents, and His will as He would want it to be done. He gave us the perfect plan in the Word of God.

When I wrote out checks on my mother's behalf, I only used her money for things I felt she wanted me to spend it on, not on things she would not personally have used her money for. We are to do the same. When we use the name of Jesus to sign our checks, so to speak, we need to make sure that it aligns to the Word of God. Jesus has given us authority to use His name on our own behalf, but we must know just how powerful His name truly is! He has trusted us by placing His own name in our hands!

Power!
Luke 22:54-63, 24:49; Acts 2; Hebrews 4:12

Jesus knew it took power for Christians to be able to stand up to all the world would throw at them on a daily basis. He also knew He wanted His children to go forth as witnesses both in their homes and in far off lands. How could they do that? Look at Peter before he was baptized in the Holy Spirit with the evidence of speaking in other tongues. (Read Luke 22:54-63 and Acts 2.) Peter could not even confess that he knew Jesus, much less preach a sermon on salvation! He was afraid. He denied even knowing Jesus three times, just as it had been foretold by Jesus, and then he went and hid. However, after Peter was baptized in the Holy Spirit, he was able to not only confess Jesus but also to stand before large crowds and preach the gospel of salvation. What a change took place in Peter's life. Jesus sent the Holy Spirit to each of us for today's power. He wants you and me to be filled with the baptism of the Holy Spirit to be able to stand strong when our own strength seems to fail us.

Jesus' last words spoken to the disciples before His ascension into the heavens were to tell the disciples to go and tarry until they were endued with power from on High. "Behold, I send the Promise of My Father upon you; but tarry in the city of Jerusalem until you are endued with power from on high" (Luke 24:49). If these were His last words on earth, then they must have been some of the most important words that were ever spoken to mankind! Jesus wants each of us to be filled with the baptism of the Holy Spirit to live a victorious and fruitful life. Have you received the baptism of the Holy Spirit with the evidence of speaking in other tongues? If so, are you praying in the Spirit often to stay tuned into the power provided through the Holy Spirit?

"For the Word of God is living and powerful, and sharper than any two-edged sword, piercing even to the division of soul and spirit, and of joints and marrow, and is a discerner of the thoughts and intents of the heart" (Heb. 4:12). Jesus gave His Word as a source of power for us to use like a tool in a warrior's hand. He said the Word of God is sharper than a two-edged sword. We must study the Word of God to be able to use this valuable tool.

We know that Jesus told us to go and tarry until we were *endued with power from on High*. We also know that He gave us the Word of God as a daily, living discerner of the thoughts and intents of the heart. The Spirit and the Word are *power*; use them daily.

The Victory!

Philippians 4:13; Romans 8:31-39; John 3:16

"I can do all things through Christ who strengthens me" (Phil. 4:13). We can only have the victory when we are in alignment with the Word of God. Whatever God asks you to do, He also provides you the tools with which to do it. Sometimes He sends along other people to help guide you to the victory, but most often, He leads you by His Word and His Spirit to complete the task He has set before you.

The conclusion to this chapter on the children's inheritance is a fulfilled life while we live and a promise one day of an eternal life in heaven. Inheritance is typically received upon the death of the loved one. But in this case, the grave could not hold our loved One, and He has already started handing out your inheritance—a victorious life!

As you read Romans 8:31-39, you will discover there is nothing that can separate you from the love of God. You are His and His alone! He loves you so much that not only did He give His only begotten Son for you (John 3:16), but He also sent the Holy Spirit to guide you through this earthly life as a source of power; a seal and guarantee of your salvation; a guide; a helper; an intercessor of the saints; and so much more. What do you need to have a victorious life? The answer will be found in the Word of God. Read the Word and you will find victory upon victory awaits you this very day.

Introspective Thinking
Isaiah 65:24

What follows will provide you with a personal time of reflection upon the many benefits you are enjoying as a Christian *right now* in your walk with Christ. The response you give today will most likely not be the response you would give tomorrow to the same question. The Lord is a current answer to your current need. He lives in the moment with you. Remember, He has already started on your answer to the problem you will carry to Him tomorrow, so relax and enjoy today's inheritance; He has tomorrow covered (Isa. 65:24).

I am enjoying the following areas of my inheritance right now:

_____

_____

_____

_____

_____

_____

_____

_____

_____

_____

_____

_____

Chapter 11

Witnessing and Living a Christian Life

Introduction
Ephesians 4:11; Mark 12:29-30; Acts 1:4-5

Living a victorious Christian life can lead you into an awesome relationship with the Lord. In addition, it can be a powerhouse for your Christian witness. Many souls can be won to the Lord simply because you choose to live a life that is filled with the love of the Lord. Preachers and teachers are called by the Lord, but all are called by the Lord to live a victorious Christian life and to be a strong witness for the Lord. (See Eph. 4:11.) We have already studied the first two commandments of the New Testament. (See Mark 12:29-30.) We know once we love the Lord our God with all that we are and then love our neighbor as our self, we are on the road to living a life that Christ intended for us to have. We have already learned that Christ commanded us to be baptized in the Holy Spirit so we could have the power we would need to be Christian witnesses in today's world. (See Acts 1:4-5.)

In this chapter, we will be speaking of the expectations of other folks concerning our walk with the Lord. What do they expect to see in someone who claims to be a Christian? Do they have certain preconceived ideas of what we as Christians look and act like?

We will look at how to be instant in season when it is not your season to bear fruit. How can you stay instant in season and out of season? Is that a trick question? Why would God expect us to be instant out of season? How can we do that?

We will also review some of our responsibilities as Christians within the church. We have already reviewed our need to take up an active role in the church body, but in this chapter we will carry this concept even further. There are many more expectations of the believer than simply our role(s) that we have been asked to perform within the church. Let's see what else is expected of us as Christians.

Being a Witness
Acts 1:8

The apostles asked Jesus, "Lord, will You at this time, restore the kingdom to Israel?" (Acts 1:8). Jesus explained to them that God did not give to them the authority over time and the seasons, but He did give to them the authority to receive the power of the Holy Spirit. He had to refocus their attention upon what He wanted them to do. He wanted them to receive the power that would be provided through the Holy Spirit for them to become witnesses of Him. Remember, these were the last words spoken by Christ to them while on earth. Right after these statements, He ascended up to the Father. Recall that last words are usually carefully chosen and should be heavily weighted by the listeners.

Parable of the Fig Tree
Mark 11:12-14; Galatians 5:22-23

Can you tell one type of tree from another tree simply by examining the leaves? I do not recognize all the various types of trees by name, but there are some trees that are so unique in their shapes and colors that I can easily identify them. For instance, the fig tree leaf has a unique shape. I can recognize a fig tree from a distance simply by the shape of the tree and the leaf. However, at a distance, it is much easier to recognize a fig tree than to predict whether there is edible fruit on the tree. The fig fruit is often out of sight, hidden under the large leaves. I would need to come close to check the tree for fruit. I also know that fig trees will only keep fruit for a short period of time before it either falls to the ground or rots on the branches. Once the fruit has gone past its season, it is no longer desirable to eat. The fruit needs to be given out to be used. It needs to be shared with all those who might desire to eat of it while it is still fresh.

Let us look at an incident in the Bible when Jesus was hungry. He saw a fig tree from across a field and crossed over the field to the tree. By the leaves He could tell it was a fig tree, and since He was hungry, He hoped that it would still have some figs on it for Him to eat. (See Mark 11:12-14.) Let us look at this in today's language. I believe Jesus used this story in the Bible to explain to the Christian how we are to be ready in season and out of season to provide fruit for the hungry. The fruit is listed in Galatians 5:22-23. In Jesus' actions, He was also demonstrating the hunger that exists in the world by both Christians and non-Christians. He shows that Christians have a responsibility to be ready to serve whoever comes to them in need at all times.

Let's look at the fig tree as a representation of a person. We can make this an exercise of learning by drawing a tree on a piece of paper. Add nine horizontal lines to the tree (within the treetop structure). Draw the tree to show deep roots within the ground. Now, using your drawing, we will begin an illustration of a person's life. Since this was a fig tree and Jesus knew it because He recognized the leaves, we can compare how others recognize us as Christians from a distance.

Create two columns at the bottom of your page under the tree's design, and under those two columns, we will begin to list characteristics that both a Christian and a non-Christian might do that are similar. For instance, both Christians and non-Christians may attend church. After all, for some folks, isn't that the thing to do? Don't good people go to church too? Churches are filled with wonderful people. Let's see what all we can brainstorm in the contrast and comparison of Christians versus non-Christians in the world or church today. We will label the characteristics that we list as leaves of the tree.

Christian Leaves	Non-Christian Leaves
– Attend church	– Attend church
– Read the Bible	– Read the Bible
– Prayer relationship	– May make attempt at prayer in public areas (for show) or for immediate help
– Clothing (outward appearance)	– Clothing (outward appearance)
– Clean language	– Clean language
– Listens to Christian music	– Could listen to Christian music
– Etc.	– Etc.

The bottom line is that both Christians and non-Christians can look very much alike from their outward appearances. It is not the leaves or the outward appearances that produce the fruit or the salvation of a person. It must be the Spirit that separates a Christian from a non-Christian.

How many times have people come up to Christians only to walk away not having been blessed by their presence? Maybe we did not try to feed their spiritual hunger. Maybe we did not have anything to give to them because we were dry and thirsty too. What a shame! Christ thought it was so much a shame that He cursed the tree for being out of season. Imagine a fig tree without a single fig to hand to the Lord. Imagine a Christian without a single Christlike fruit to give out to someone who is hungry. How sad!

Be Instant
2 Timothy 3:16-17, 4:2

Second Timothy 3:16-17 says, "All Scripture is given by inspiration of God, and is profitable for doctrine, for reproof, for correction, for instruction in righteousness, that the man of God may be complete, thoroughly equipped for every good work." The reason Timothy could encourage you to preach the Word and to be ready both in season and out of season (2 Tim. 4:2) is because he understood that when you stay in the Word of God, you will be able to feel complete and to give out even when the times are tough. Even if you are asked to give in your out-of-season time, Timothy understood there are no shortages of fruit when you stay complete in God's Word.

Now think of a gardener who has diligently gathered in the fruits of his labor and preserved them by canning or freezing the produce for later use. When you store the Word of God, the Holy Spirit, and the love of Jesus, you can go to the pantry of your spiritual life and pull out what is needed to share with others when the time arises. You cannot build up your spiritual pantry until you have stayed in the Word of God and stayed in the presence of the Lord. Being instant out of season is possible only by storing up God's goodness in your life. When you do not stay current in your relationship with Christ, your ability to cultivate the faith of others is lessened; one cannot nourish the hungry with spoiled fruit. Then others will leave your presence hungry. Once again, how sad!

Bearing Fruit
Galatians 5:22-23

Jesus went to the fig tree for fruit. Let's look at the fruit of the Spirit (this is where you will list the fruit of the Spirit on the nine lines I asked you to place within your tree top diagram).

- love
- joy
- peace
- longsuffering
- kindness
- goodness
- faithfulness
- gentleness
- self-control

Christ says there is no law against the fruit of the Spirit. As discussed in chapter 10, the fruit of the Spirit cannot be stolen from us. There is no need for a law to be written to protect the fruit; it is forever protected by God's Word. The fruit is blessed and can be used in abundance. Not only do you need the fruit to manifest itself within your own life, but you will also be able to serve others even in what would appear to be your out-of-season time.

Can you think of an out-of-season time for a Christian? How about the death of a loved one? That is hard, and it is difficult to minister to others when we are personally grieving, yet I have seen time and again when a Christian I came to minister to because of his great loss was actually ministering to all those who came to pay their respects to his loved one. Where did that strength come from? It came from the stored-up fruit of the Spirit. It came from the promises of God that He will never leave us. It came from the presence of the Lord. We can minister when in the natural (carnal) we might want to declare a personal pity party. God gives us strength to minister even in the hardest of times.

Give Me Just One More Year
Mark 11:12-14; Luke 13:6-9; Hebrews 9:27

Once again taking the two parables of the fig tree from the Scriptures found in Luke 13:6-9 and Mark 11:12-14, I have often wondered if the two stories were somehow tied together. Follow with me as we read of the story in Luke of the land owner telling the vineyard master that because the fig tree had produced no fruit for the past three years, he was to cut it down, and the story in Mark of the Lord cursing the fig tree because it had no fruit. Were these two trees possibly the same fig tree? Hmm, I wonder if these two stories are related.

Let's look at it as though it were one continuous story for a moment. In Luke the vineyard master begs the owner to allow him one more year to give the tree an in-depth work of digging, fertilizing, and pruning. He told the master if it still did not produce fruit, he would release the tree to the owner of the field to be cut down. Now follow along with me in my vision of these two fig tree parables. The owner of the field had come by for three years and seen no productivity from the tree. The master asked the vineyard master, "Why does it use up the ground?" (Luke 13:7).

The parable in Luke ends there, but let us assume that the vineyard master was actually given the extension of one or possibly as many as three years to work on the fig tree. Now, we move on to the parable in Mark. The Lord (owner of the field) is hungry, and He sees the tree that He has granted a year, two, or even three years extension already. He goes over to the tree in anticipation of receiving some fruit from the tree. Surely by now the tree should be bearing fruit! There is none. Per the agreement between the vineyard master and the owner of the field, the tree is cursed and dies overnight. The tree never produced any fruit.

Taking this concept into our personal lives, how often do we pray for a loved one or friend to be given more time and mercy from the Lord while we pray that the Holy Spirit might somehow reach them and show them that they need the Lord in their lives? We spend time trying to speak to them, and the Holy Spirit begins to dig around and fertilize them. God does not want anyone to be lost and or to be cut down, but there is an appointed day for each and every one of us. "And as it is appointed for men to die once" (Heb. 9:27).

Also think of the times when you have felt as though there were situations in your own life that hurt. We may find ourselves blaming God for these hurtful or painful situations. However, sometimes He is only digging around us and fertilizing us to make us more productive. I cannot imagine that a rose bush enjoys being pruned, dug around, fertilized, sprayed for bugs, etc. It all must cause some discomfort, but once this painful process has been completed, the rose bush typically begins to produce beautiful and aromatic roses—the kinds of roses that make visitors want to walk over to touch and smell. However, if the rose bush does not produce roses over a period of time, the owner will most likely replace it with another bush that is willing and able to produce beautiful roses. After all, the bush is just taking up space in his beautiful flower garden.

Are you producing fruit that causes others to want to come closer to examine your spiritual life? Do you draw others to the Lord? Or do you push them away even further? Sometimes we need to be fertilized, even if it stinks at the time! Be patient, and submit to the Master of your field. He will only do things that will make you better and more beautiful in His sight.

Bible Study and Prayer
2 Timothy 2:15; John 14:14

Bible study should be done on a regular basis. Paul said to "Be diligent to present yourself approved to God, a worker who does not need to be ashamed, rightly dividing the word of truth" (2 Tim. 2:15). Establish a daily time for yourself to study God's Word. Do you have a daily time to go to work? Do you have a daily set time to get up and do certain chores around the house? Make sure that you have included your time with the Lord. He should never be left out of a single day.

How often we leave the very one who made the day just for us out of our lives. If your spouse or close friend made a special gift for you and watched you throw it away, wouldn't you think it might offend and hurt him? Jesus made today for you. He has a plan to bless you on this very day. Be sure to include Him in the sharing of the day He has made for you. It just makes good sense to me to start off by speaking to the Creator of the day instead of trying to second guess the plans of the day. He will show you what you need for today when you read His plan, the Word.

Prayer is simply talking with God the Father. Believers are to pray through Jesus, using His name in prayer. "If you ask anything in My name, I will do it" (John 14:14). Prayer is your communication with the Lord through the Holy Spirit. Once again, how sad it is to think that you could spend an entire day without talking to the One you said you love the most! But the distractions of life can frequently keep you from spending time with those you care for the most. To live a victorious life, you must be about your Father's business, and to do that, you need to know the Lord in His fullness. Spend time worshipping and listening to the Lord in daily prayer. If you need to know how to pray, think of it this way: He is your best friend. How do you talk to your best friend? Talk to Jesus the same way.

Church Attendance
Hebrews 10:24-25

Christian fellowship, singing, worshipping, and the study of God's Word only help to strengthen the Christian in his walk with the Lord. "And let us consider one another in order to stir up love and good works, not forsaking the assembling of ourselves together, as is the manner of some, but exhorting one another, and so much the more as you see the Day approaching" (Heb. 10:24-25). The Lord desires for us to come together as a body of believers to edify and strengthen one another in our testimony and worship to the Lord. How beautiful it is to see an entire body of believers worshipping the Lord. I would imagine that even angels are listening and joining in. They cannot sing the songs of salvation, but certainly they can sing with joy over our salvation.

Hold on to Your Confession
Hebrews 10:11-25; 2 Peter 3:17-18

Read Hebrews 10:11-25. Note that Hebrews 10:14 says, "For by one offering He has perfected forever those who are being sanctified." Many times we do not hold onto our confession because we tend to forget what Jesus has done for us. He has paid the price once and for all.

Second Peter 3:17-18 states, "You therefore, beloved, since you know this beforehand, beware lest you also fall from your own steadfastness, being led away with the error of the wicked; but grow in the grace and knowledge of our Lord and Savior Jesus Christ. To Him be the glory both now and forever. Amen." The Lord wants you to grow in knowledge of Him. You must study God's Word, attend a solid Word of God–based church, develop friendships with other believers, and maintain a powerful prayer life to grow in His knowledge.

Be Dependable
Colossians 3:9, 17

When you commit yourself to something, you need to follow through with it. It is so annoying to have people tell me they are going to do something or be someplace at a prearranged time and date only to find they forgot, got busy, or changed their minds. Do any of these phrases sound familiar? Hopefully you are not the one saying them! God expects His children to stand by what they say. He sets the example for us to live by. We are damaging our witness to others when we do not follow through with our commitments. Colossians 3:17 says, "And whatever you do in word or deed, do all in the name of the Lord Jesus, giving thanks to God the Father through Him." We make commitments to others as unto the Lord, and we need to follow through just as He would follow through for us.

Paul tells us, "Do not lie to one another, since you have put off the old man with his deeds" (Col. 3:9). There are things that happen to us that we never would have planned on that can cause us to have unforeseen schedule changes. It is at those times when we need to make very sure we have contacted all those who might be affected by our own issues and inform them we cannot follow through with our commitment to them. They will most likely be grateful for your honesty and thankful that you communicated to them early on in your dilemma.

When you make commitments to others, you should always be on time, prepared, and thoroughly equipped to handle the commitment. This includes church attendance. When you agree to become a church member, you need to follow through with your actions, making sure that church attendance, punctuality, tithes and offerings, and service to others is a central part of your commitment to the church and to the Lord.

Give of Your Tithes and Offerings
Malachi 3:8-11

Refer back to some of the notes from chapter 8 on tithes and offerings. *Bringing all the tithes into the storehouse* refers to the church where you are being spiritually feed. The Lord loves a cheerful giver, and so does the pastor! A giver is not a director of the money given either. Make sure that when you give your tithes and offerings, it is not for show, manipulation, or personal credit. Pretend no one is watching you give other than the Lord. In many churches, this is very close to the truth. In many churches, this is very close to the truth. There are some pastors who frequently do not want to know who is giving and who is not. A pastor may ask the church treasurer to not inform him if there are members who are not tithing or giving. Being informed about the members who tithe and those who do not is a personal decision available to each pastor.

Respect for Your Leaders in the Church
1 Thessalonians 5:12-13; Hebrews 13:7, 17

The pastor of the church is a person God has placed within the church as an undershepherd of tremendous responsibility over the Lord's sheep (Christians). We as the flock are to respect all of the Lord's anointed workers He has placed to be over us. "And we urge you, brethren, to recognize those who labor among you, and are over you in the Lord and admonish you, and to esteem them very highly in love for their work's sake. Be at peace among yourselves" (1 Thess. 5:12-13).

The Lord is so gracious to give us spiritual leaders, who we often refer to as our spiritual mothers and fathers in the Lord. Jesus wants us to "Remember those who rule over you, who have spoken the Word of God to you, whose faith follow, considering the outcome of their conduct" (Heb. 3:7). You are to remember and respect those God has placed over you in your Christian walk, but you are also to examine or *consider* the outcome of their conduct. Once again, it comes right back to our Christian conduct. If a pastor or church leader exhibits Christlike behavior and gives you the pure, undivided Word of God, then follow him in his faith. But the test the Lord has given to you is clear: watch your leaders' conduct. Even those over you must be accountable to God, and their lives must align to the Word of God. You are to be respectful and follow in their path only if they live their lives according to the Word of God.

"Obey those who rule over you, and be submissive, for they watch out for your souls, as those who must give account. Let them do so with joy and not with grief for that would be unprofitable for you" (Heb. 13:17). Their responsibility to you is to be obedient to the Lord concerning how they shepherd the people. Your responsibility to them is to always hold them up in prayer and to follow through with all the commitments that you make to them or to the church body. You should be submissive and respectful to those who rule over you in the Lord. Always have a Christlike spirit toward the leaders in the Church. You are not to give them *grief*!

Finally

Witnessing and living a Christian life should be a daily event for you. Wake up each day with a new agenda from the Lord. Who will He send your way today? Will you have the fruit of the Spirit ready to give out as needed? Will you be committed to fulfilling all you have signed up for in your family, church, and career? Will you seek out your service for the Lord in the church and the world for today? Will you strive for a personal growth in the Lord this day?

Salvation is for everyone. God wants all His children to be about the Father's business—witnessing and living a Christian life so others may know Him.

⤚ Chapter 12 ⤙

The Rapture

Introduction

In this chapter, we will discuss the rapture of the Church and the importance of living a Christian life. Christ is returning for His bride, the born-again believers. The day and the hour of His return are unknown to man. Therefore, it is critical that we hold fast to our confession of faith and not waver in our Christian walk with the Lord.

We will review some personal questions that will help you to measure your own walk with the Lord. Are you truly growing in the faith or simply holding on to past memories and experiences of your salvation? Our God is a God of today. Yesterday is history and tomorrow is uncertain, but one thing is certain: God loves you and desires that you love Him too. Stay ready to meet the One who loves you the most.

Natural versus Spiritual Bodies
1 Corinthians 15:44-49; John 3:3, 6:63, 14:6; John 3:3

There is a basic understanding that must be spoken of at this point. First Corinthians 15:44-46, 49 reads:

> It is sown a natural body, it is raised a spiritual body. There is a natural body, and there is a spiritual body. And so it is written, "The first man Adam became a living being." The last Adam

became a life-giving spirit. However, the spiritual is not first, but the natural, and afterward the spiritual. And as we have borne the image of the man of dust, we shall also bear the image of the heavenly Man.

The first Adam bore the image of the *man of dust*, and the second Adam, Christ, bore the image of the *heavenly Man*. We have already read in chapter 2 concerning salvation that man must be born again to see the kingdom of God (John 3:3). We need to understand that the spiritual man is just as ever present and real in us as our earthly bodies are to us. We can see with our earthly eyes our own hands and feet, but we often struggle to grasp the reality that our spiritual man was made in the image of the *heavenly man* and is not born within us until we accept the Lord Jesus as our personal Savior. It is easy to fall into the trap of believing only what we can see and touch, but Christ has given the plan of salvation, our second birth, to each of us so we might be ready to experience the rapture of the Church.

Prior to your second birth, you have a spirit of the world within you that is doomed to eternal death. You are born with a spirit, but the spirit has not been birthed into life until you accept Jesus as your personal Savior. You must be born again to have life created within your spirit. Jesus declared, "I am the way, the truth, and the life. No one comes to the Father except through Me" (John 14:6). Without salvation, you have a dead spirit within you.

"It is the Spirit who gives life; the flesh profits nothing" (John 6:63). Your flesh is destined to return to dust, but your spirit was originally destined to live eternally with God the Father, Son, and Holy Spirit. By accepting the Lord as your personal Savior, you are simply putting your spiritual life back into the original plan God had for you from the start.

The Rapture Is Reality
1 Thessalonians 4:13-18

Have you ever planned a vacation? Did you read all about the place you were traveling to? Did you plan your wardrobe to fit the location of your travels? Did you tell others about the excitement of your upcoming trip? Did you have trouble going to sleep at night because your mind was on the anticipated trip? If you can relate to these questions, then you are on the tip of the level of excitement we should feel at the very mention of the coming of the Lord!

I contend that the rapture is not taught nowadays nearly as often as it was in years prior. We have become cold to the fact that Jesus never lies. If He said He would return, *He will return*. Therefore, we need to be rejoicing and looking for the day our Lord and Savior will return for His own. We are lulled into the cares of this life, which only serve to deaden our senses to the signs that are all around us. The whole earth cries out that our Lord is ready to return for His bride.

> But I do not want you to be ignorant, brethren, concerning those who have fallen asleep, lest you sorrow as others who have no hope. For if we believe that Jesus died and rose again, even so God will bring with Him those who sleep in Jesus. For this we say to you by the word of the Lord, that we who are alive and remain until the coming of the Lord will by no means precede those who are asleep. For the Lord Himself will descend from heaven with a shout, with the voice of an archangel, and with the trumpet of God. And the dead in Christ will rise first. Then we who are alive and remain shall be caught up together with them in the clouds to meet the Lord in the air. And thus we shall always be with the Lord. Therefore comfort one another with these words (1 Thess. 4:13-18).

It is possible that you, or someone you know, have never heard of the rapture. It is important to understand the concept of the rapture in both a scriptural and visual way so you can burn it deep within your spirit. Blink your eyes to see how quickly God will transform your mortal body for the rapture. The Scripture says the believer will be changed in a *twinkling of an eye*.

Maybe one of the reasons we do not go around talking about the rapture is simply because we know so little about it. We cannot look it up on one of the many travel channels on television, map finders on our computer, or other such helpful electronic tools of today's time. But the Lord has given us enough information in the Bible so we can know that it is going to be above and beyond all our minds can comprehend. It will be like nothing we have ever known before. Let us look at what the Word of God says about the rapture.

The First Family Reunion
1 Thessalonians 4:13-18

First Thessalonians 4:17 says, "Caught up together with them." As a body of believers, both the dead in Christ and those who are alive in Christ will be joined together in the sky to meet our Lord. This is the rapture, and it is, in my interpretation, the first family reunion. The Word of God tells me that my parents, who both loved the Lord with all their hearts and have been buried for many years, will rise first into the air. Next it says, "Then we who are alive and remain shall be caught up together with them in the clouds to meet the Lord in the air." This tells me I will be *caught up together* with my parents in the air so we will go as one to meet the Lord.

The dead in Christ (Christians who have died before us) have the advantage of rising first, but the Lord does not play favorites, so He allows Christians who are alive and remain on the earth to catch up with the dead in Christ. We will travel to meet the Lord in the air together. It is thrilling to think of seeing my loved ones once again. My heart begins to skip a beat at the mere thought of seeing the family members I have already had to say good-bye to while on this earth. But it does not compare to the thrill and excitement I feel over the fact I will get to finally see my Lord face to face! What a day that will be! Can you imagine the joy, excitement, and thrill of so much happiness all happening at once? We would have to have a glorified body just to be able to contain this much excitement!

How Will He Take Us?

1 Corinthians 15:50-58; John 3:3, 14:1-6; 1 Thessalonians 5:1-11; Luke 21:34-36; James 5:7-8

Paul refers to the rapture as a *mystery*: "I tell you a mystery: We shall not all sleep, but we shall all be changed" (1 Cor. 15:51). The rapture is a *mystery* simply because we have not experienced it. We are told in Scripture that the rapture will occur in a moment, in the twinkling of an eye.

I can almost understand the phrase, *in the twinkling of an eye* by using my own mother's death as a comparison. I got the privilege of being beside my dear mother as she drew her last breath here on earth. Life and death were simply one breath apart. One moment she was breathing and the next moment she was not. She crossed over to life everlasting in the twinkling of an eye! Christ tells us our transition into the heavens will be just that quick for all believers. Just imagine as you blink your eyes not only you, but *all* Christians on the entire face of the earth will be caught up together in the clouds to meet the Lord. What a miracle!

We know the transition will be quick—*in a twinkling of an eye*. Now let us look at the events that occur almost simultaneously. The Bible tells us the *last trumpet* will sound. Those who have died will rise first, and then we who are still alive shall also be changed and meet them in the air as we go together to be with the Lord forever.

Where Will He Take Us?

1 Thessalonians 4:14; John 14:1-6

Paul also tells us in 1 Thessalonians 4:14, "For if we believe that Jesus died and rose again, even so God will bring with Him those who sleep in Jesus." I believe somehow when the last trumpet sounds and Jesus returns for His bride, God will be in charge of bringing the dead in Christ (or those who sleep in Christ) to the meeting in the air. Paul refers to it as a *mystery*, and I can only agree with his choice of words. But just as Paul said that we are to comfort one another with these words of the wonderful upcoming mystery of the rapture, I will write about it, teach it, and talk about it to anyone who will listen until He returns. Oh, how the rich man wanted Lazarus (John 14:1-6) to return to earth to tell his family of the reality of the second birth! Let us tell as many people as we can about the coming of Christ and our wonderful gift of salvation.

Where Will My Mansion Be in Heaven?
Luke 16:19-31; John 14:1-6; Acts 10:34

Jesus tells us in the book of John that He is going to heaven to prepare for us a place in His Father's mansion. In fact, He says, "In My Father's house are many mansions: if it were not so, I would have told you. I go to prepare a place for you" (John 14:2). I have heard over and over that Jesus is going to prepare a mansion for the believers. That may well be the case. However, let us read this Scripture as it is written. It says "in my Father's house are many mansions . . . I go to prepare a place for you." I have been married to my dear husband for over forty years, and he did not prepare a place for me, once we were married, that was down the street from his house. My husband sought out a home we could share as one. I do not believe Christ ever intended for us to live apart. We are often referred to as the bride of Christ. He desires to have us close to Him—not to ever have to live apart from Him.

To give you another personal analogy, I am a parent of two beautiful daughters. They have great husbands, and I am blessed to have six wonderful grandchildren. When they come to my house, I prepare them a place within my home. I interpret this Scripture to say the Lord is going to prepare a place for us *in* His Father's house. In fact, the rooms or places are so big that He referred to them as mansions! I believe, as children of God, we will all live in the Father's house, but we will not have tiny bedrooms; we will have enormous living suites that are like mansions. Think about it. Our God made the entire universe. Making a very large house to hold all of His children is certainly not too big a concept for Him.

Another way to look at this idea is to ask yourself this question: which one of your children will you choose to assign to live down the street from you or even miles away from you? And which of the children will get to live inside your house? The Bible tells us He is no respecter of persons (Acts 10:34). Therefore, He would clearly have a difficult time deciding which of the children get to live down the street and which ones get to live inside the house. He certainly could not go by the alphabet; we all have the same last name—His!

I do not see where one child will get a smaller place than another. I believe we will each have a beautiful home within the house of God that is prepared with us in mind. When we have family come to stay for a few days, we prepare a place for them. Making sure the rooms look like what we think they would need and desire is a priority for us. We are excited and anticipate their arrival. We love having them stay with us. Jesus has gone away to prepare a special place for us to live right in the home of the Father. I truly believe it is on His mind always that we will soon be joining Him in the Father's house.

Occupy Till He Comes
1 Corinthians 11:26; 2 Peter 3:18

In essence, occupy till He comes means going about in our daily lives as if the rapture were to occur *today*. What will you be doing the day/the moment of the rapture? We should be watching always for the rapture to occur. Why? Because He will surely come for His people. We must examine ourselves in the following areas:

- Will He find you ready to face Him in a twinkling of an eye?
- Are you staying current with your relationship with the Lord?
- Are you reading the Bible?
- Are you praying daily?
- Are you attending church regularly?
- Are you paying your tithes and offerings regularly?
- Are you witnessing to others?
- Are you loving your neighbors as yourself?
- Are you loving your brothers and sisters in the Lord?

- Are you growing in the grace and knowledge of your Lord Jesus Christ (2 Peter 3:18)?

These are all important aspects of your daily walk with the Lord. He will help you to hunger after Christian fellowship and to hunger after His Word if you ask Him. The church you attend should be a Bible-based church, and it should teach belief in the Word of God from Genesis through Revelation. I encourage you to attend a church where you feel the presence of the Lord, where you see the fruit of the Spirit manifest, and where you truly believe the Lord has directed you to attend. You will experience a satisfaction in being supported in love by your Christian brothers and sisters. You will also be a blessing to many in need of your support as you serve the Lord together as the body of Christ.

Be Patient!
James 5:7-10; Matthew 24:36

> Therefore be patient, brethren, until the coming of the Lord. See, how the farmer waits for the precious fruit of the earth, waiting patiently for it, until he receives the early and latter rain. You also be patient. Establish your heart, for the coming of the Lord is at hand. Do not grumble against one another, brethren, lest you be condemned. Behold, the Judge is standing at the door! My brethren, take the prophets, who spoke in the name of the Lord, as an example of suffering and patience. Indeed, we count them blessed who endure. You have heard of the perseverance of Job and seen the end intended by the Lord—that the Lord is very compassionate and merciful (James 5:7-10).

James tells believers to be patient. Our heavenly Father has His own timing and His own reasons for holding the rapture back another minute. We who are ready are eagerly awaiting His return, but we must understand the sovereignty of God. He is longsuffering and patient. He is truth and will come again as He told us; we are to eagerly wait for Him.

The Scripture tells us He, the Judge, is *waiting at the door*. That's how close His coming is! We need to recognize His coming is sooner than we think.

Even when our lives are going through trials and tribulations (like Job's life), we should follow Job's example and hold fast to our own profession of faith. The Lord will come for a spotless bride. Will you be ready?

No Christian Misses the Rapture!
1 Thessalonians 4:16

One day this revelation hit me and got me to wondering if it is even spoken of very often among the body of believers. Just because someone has died (*asleep in the Lord*) does *not* prevent him or her from experiencing the rapture. Think about it. First Thessalonians 4:16 says, "And the dead in Christ shall rise first." I have heard many sermons on the rapture concerning how we do not want to miss it, but the preacher is really referring to whether we are saved or not saved.

We, the living, will not be the only ones going up at the time of the rapture. We have no need to sorrow over the loss of our loved ones if they are born-again believers in Jesus Christ. They are resting in and enjoying the presence of the Lord in a depth we have yet to attain. God will bring them at the time of the rapture. For those of us who remain, we too will be changed in a twinkling of an eye, and we will all meet together with the Lord in the air. Thus we shall ever be with the Lord. What a day that will be! These are truly comforting words from the Lord.

Rapture and the Second Coming
The book of Revelation

The rapture and the second coming of Christ are *two* different occurrences. The book of Revelation gives more insight into the second coming and the descriptions of heaven.

Christ will return *to the earth* in the second coming versus His return into the clouds at the rapture. It is not the intent of this chapter to give an in-depth study on the second coming, only to make it clear that the two occurrences are distinct and separate. I believe the born-again believer in

Jesus Christ will be raptured out of this earth and this event will usher in the many events of the tribulation, the great tribulation, and the second coming of Christ. There are many more mysteries as you study the wonderful workings of God for the days ahead that are for Christians. The second coming will not be a time to be feared by the Christian but certainly will be a fearful and awful time for nonbelievers. I choose to be ready for the rapture and to allow Christ to have control over the events of the tribulation and the second coming.

Are You Ready?
Romans 10:8-13; 1 Peter 1:3-10

It is my prayer that this book has brought you into a deeper understanding of the Scriptures in one or more areas of your life. It is certainly my prayer that if you have not accepted Jesus Christ as your personal Lord and Savior that you will do so now. It only takes a moment to be birthed into the kingdom of God, and then you will begin to experience all the benefits He has bestowed upon His children.

If you would like to accept Jesus as your personal Savior, please repeat this simple prayer to the Lord.

> Dear Jesus, please forgive me of my sins, wash me clean, and create in me a new heart. I now confess You as my personal Savior and Lord of my life. I give my life to You completely. I believe that You died upon the cross for my sins. I believe God raised You from the dead and that You dwell with Him. I will serve You all the days of my life. Amen.

Jesus will forgive you of all your sins, cleanse you, and make you feel like a new person in Him. You will experience a spiritual birth that will breathe life into your soul. You are now ready for the rapture, but more importantly, you are now ready to begin to *live*! Congratulations!

CPSIA information can be obtained at www.ICGtesting.com
Printed in the USA
LVOW080831310812

296593LV00001B/2/P